# Seashells in My Pocket
## Second edition

## A Child's Nature Guide to Exploring the Atlantic Coast

by Judith Hansen
illustrated by Donna Sabaka

APPALACHIAN MOUNTAIN CLUB BOOKS
BOSTON, MASSACHUSETTS

Illustrations by Donna Sabaka
Book design by Carol Bast Tyler
Cover design by Joyce Weston

© Copyright 1992 by Judith Hansen

Published by Appalachian Mountain Club Books, 5 Joy Street, Boston, MA 02108

Distributed by The Globe Pequot Press, Inc., Old Saybrook, CT 06475

*Library of Congress Cataloging-in-Publication Data*
Hansen, Judith. 1944–
    Seashells in my pocket: a child's guide to exploring the Atlantic Coast / by Judith Hansen: illustrated by Donna Sabaka. —Rev. and expanded ed.
        p.  cm.
    Includes index.
    Summary: A guide to the plants and animals that may be found along the Atlantic shore from Maine to Florida.
    ISBN 1-878239-15-5: $10.95
    1. Seashore fauna—Atlantic Coast (U.S.)—Identification—Juvenile literature. 2. Seashore flora—Atlantic Coast (U.S.)—Identification—Juvenile literature. [1. Seashore biology—Atlantic Coast (U.S.)] I. Sabaka, Donna R., ill. II. Title.
QH104.5.A84H36    1992
574974'09146—dc20                  92-24397
                                             CIP
                                             AC

The paper used in this publication meets the minimum requirements of the American National Standard for Information Sciences—Permanence of Paper for Printed Library Materials, ANSI Z39.48-1984.∞

Printed on recycled paper. ♲

Printed in the United States of America.

10 9 8 7 6 5 4 3

# Contents

Seashells in My Pocket *is dedicated
to our children, Amy, Jason, and Justin,
and to young sea-searchers everywhere.*

# Preface

*Seashells in My Pocket* was written for children ages six and up who like the seashore. In using this guidebook, children will learn not only the names of many plants and animals, but where and how they live. Older children will be able to use this book by themselves, either as a guide for exploring the coast or as a resource for school projects. Younger children can enjoy this book with the help of an adult. Although the language is simple, the book should be of interest to adults as well.

Children enjoy a challenge, but they thrive on achievement. Care has been taken to include only those species that are common along the Atlantic coast, so that readers will be encouraged when completing the checklist at the back of the book. A Sea-Searcher's Award is also included. It can be filled in after the reader has identified all the plants and animals on the list.

The text and illustrations are organized to make it easy for children to compare the different species and to distinguish one from the other. Rule marks are printed on the back cover to help the children make field identifications.

Everyone loves pretty seashells, and this book includes a section about shells that may be collected. The emphasis, however, is on enjoying and identifying coastal plants and animals where they are, disturbing the environment as little as possible. We hope that the adults who use this book with their children or students will reinforce that message.

There is always something new to learn when visiting the seashore. *Seashells in My Pocket* can be the beginning of a lifetime of exploring and learning about the seashore and about nature.

# 1. Exploring the Seashore

Thousands of plants and animals live on the coast and in the sea. The plants and animals described in this book are easy to find along the Atlantic coast of the United States from Maine to Florida. Some of them can be seen inland, away from the coast, and in other places in North America. A few may be found on or near other oceans. The map that appears with each species in this book shows where, along the Atlantic coast, the plant or animal can be seen.

Just as some plants and animals can live only in fresh water, others must live in seawater. For example, if you took a trout from a lake and put it in the ocean it would die. If you took a crab from the ocean and put it in a lake, the crab would die. This is not true of all animals and plants, but it is true of most things that live in water.

It is also true that different plants and animals live in different oceans of the world, and even in different parts of the same ocean. Some ocean life needs deep, cold water; some needs shallow, warm water. Some living things make their homes in the rocks, others in the sand or mud or dune grass.

If you live near the ocean or have ever visited the ocean, you might have noticed that the ocean seems to be moving all the time. And it is. Twice each day, the water slowly moves up the shore and then slowly moves back out. Seawater that has reached its highest point on the land is called *high tide*. Seawater at its lowest point is called *low tide*.

The best time to explore the coast is at low tide. The ocean leaves shells, seaweed, and other treasures behind as it goes out. Many shorebirds come to feed on the small plants and animals. Tide pools, which are pools of water left among the rocks and in low places on the beach when the tide goes out, are full of living plants and animals to watch.

There are clues to help you identify every type of plant or animal that you find. You can identify a plant or animal by its color, size, shape, and the place where you find it. You can also identify an animal by the way it acts, which is called its *behavior*. It helps to compare the animals or plants with each other.

At the back of this book is a list of plants and animals you can find on the Atlantic coast. The next time you visit the coast, check off each plant, animal, and shell that you see. When you have found everything on the list, cut out the Sea-Searcher's

Award, fill in your name, and hang the award on your wall or put it in a scrapbook.

Exploring the coast and beachcombing are fun all year long. Coastal plants are beautiful even without their flowers. You can see different kinds of shorebirds by visiting the same place on the coast at different times of the year. One of the best times to find plant and animal treasures from the sea is after a winter storm.

Most explorers need some equipment and special clothing. They also have rules to protect themselves, the places they explore, and the wildlife they study.

## What to Wear

1. Sneakers (not your best ones!) or other rubber-soled shoes. They will protect your feet and keep you from slipping on the rocks.
2. A jacket or shirt with pockets, in which you can put shells that might break easily.
3. On sunny days, sunglasses or a hat with a visor to protect your eyes.
4. If you're exploring in wooded areas, wear long pants, tucked into your socks, to protect yourself from ticks.

## What to Take

1. A friend. It's safer—and more fun—to go exploring with a buddy or a grown-up.
2. Insect spray and sunscreen lotion.

3. A plastic bag to collect samples of plants and shells. Remember, only take one sample of each and don't collect living animals or whole living plants.

4. A pencil and a drawing pad if you like to draw pictures.

5. A magnifying glass for taking closer looks at tiny plants and creatures.

6. Binoculars for a closer view of birds.

7. A pair of scissors (with safe, rounded points) for cutting small pieces of seaweed or live plants.

8. This guidebook.

9. A backpack to carry everything, so your hands will be free for picking up samples and for climbing on the rocks.

## Some Safety Rules

1. *Undertow.* In some places along the coast there are strong currents that can pull you quickly out into deep water. If you are exploring a part of the coast where you have never been before, you or a grown-up can check with a lifeguard or a police officer to find out if there is anything special you should know about the area.

2. *Slippery rocks.* Rocks that are covered with seaweed are very slippery. Even rocks that look bare are often covered with tiny plants called algae that are also very slippery. Your rubber-soled shoes will help, but be careful where you step. Never walk out onto rocks where the waves are crashing. Big waves are beautiful and exciting, but they can knock a person over in a flash.

3. *The tides.* Sometimes sandy or rocky points that you can walk to at low tide become islands when the tide comes in. Such places are fun to explore, but you don't want to get stranded. So before you begin, find out if the tide is going out or coming in. In every town along the coast, you can get a chart that shows when the tide will be low and when it will be high. The local newspaper usually prints a tide chart, and you can often find a tide chart at a supermarket or library or at the police station. The times for high tide and low tide change each day, so be sure to check.

## Some Rules to Protect the Environment

1. Never collect live animals or whole living plants. You will find many empty shells, shells with dead animals in them, and pieces of seaweed tossed up on the beach and rocks. If you need a sample of a living plant or of a large clump of seaweed, use your scissors to snip off a small piece.

2. When collecting shells, take only one of each type. Even the dead plants and animals are an important part of seashore life. They become food and shelter for living animals.

3. When exploring sand dunes, walk only on marked paths. Dune grass, which is very fragile, helps keep the sand from blowing away. Also, some birds make their nests in the dune grass.

4. When picking up a live animal for a closer look, handle it gently. There are special hints about handling live animals in the chapters that follow.

5. In addition to the treasures of the coast, you will find trash that people have tossed from boats or left at the beach. If you take a snack along, make sure you don't leave any trash behind. (Treats for the gulls are okay.) Some beachcombers take along an extra plastic bag. They help keep the beach clean by picking up some trash and throwing it in a trash bin on the beach or taking it home with them. You can help clean up the seashore if you pick up trash left by others, too.

# 2. Sea Creatures

In this chapter, you will find out about living animals that you can see on the coast. The size given for each animal is that of an adult. Many of the animals you see will not be full grown and so they will be smaller than the size listed. But you will be able to identify the animals by reading about them and by looking at the illustrations.

## Starfish

It is easy to identify starfish, or sea stars, as they are sometimes called. They look like stars. A starfish is not a fish, though. It does not have gills or fins. And it does not have a skeleton. It is soft underneath, and the top of its body has a tough covering that feels like leather.

Starfish live on the bottom of the ocean in both deep and shallow water. Sometimes dead starfish are washed up on the beach, but you can often see living starfish in tide pools. On the south coast they live along sandy shores and in coral reefs. They may not be moving or even look as if they are alive. But if you pick up a starfish and turn it over (handle the starfish gently), it will probably wave some of its feet at you. Underneath each arm are hundreds of tiny suction-cup feet that the starfish uses to move along the rocks or sand and to hold its food.

At the end of each arm you will see an orange eyespot. A starfish can't see, but it can sense light and dark with its eyespots. In the center of the starfish, you will see a small circle. That is the starfish's mouth, which it uses in a very unusual way. To eat its favorite food, a mussel or a clam, the starfish wraps its arms around the animal's shell and pulls it open a little way. Then the starfish pushes its stomach out of its body through its mouth and into the open shell. It digests the animal, then slides its stomach out of the empty shell and back inside its own body.

After you have finished looking at the starfish, put it back in the water. A starfish can live out of the water for only a few minutes. Most starfish included in this book have five arms. The **Slender Sea Star** might have six arms. The **Smooth Sun Star,** which looks like a sunflower, can have from seven to fourteen arms. Sometimes you might see a starfish with one or two arms missing because of a fight or an accident, but don't worry. This animal can grow (regenerate) a new arm.

# Cushion Star

*Color:* adults are red, orange, or yellow; young are green or dark purple

*Size:* 10 inches across

The largest sea star on the Atlantic coast is the **Cushion Star.** Its fat body is covered on top with a pattern of ridges that looks like a net. Try counting all the squares and triangles!

# Thorny Sea Star

*Color:* purple, red, or orange

*Size:* 8 inches across

Look for the **Thorny Sea Star** on sunny days because it is attracted to light. Its small body is covered with rows of large spines.

# Slender Sea Star

*Color:* red, pink, lavender, or purple

*Size:* 3 inches across

The **Slender Sea Star** has long, narrow arms. The **Northern Sea Star** has a soft, fat body; on top of each arm, there is a thin row of tiny spines that looks like a white line. The Slender, Northern, and **Forbes's Common** sea stars are bumpy on top. The **Blood Star** and the **Smooth Sun Star** are smooth. The colors listed with each type of starfish tell the color of the top of that starfish.

# Blood Star

*Color:* red, pink, purple, orange, yellow, or white

*Size:* 8 inches across (from the tip of one point to the tip of the opposite point)

# Forbes's Common Sea Star

*Color:* tan, brown, or olive green

*Size:* 10 inches across

# Northern Sea Star

*Color:* orange, pink, gray, tan, lavender, or blue

*Size:* 16 inches across

# Smooth Sun Star

*Color:* purple, red, pink, or orange

*Size:* 16 inches across

### Sea Urchin

A living sea urchin is covered with long spines that it uses in two ways. Bits of seaweed that stick to the spines help the sea urchin hide from its enemies. The sea urchin also uses the spines on its underside to move along the sand or rocks. You can find live sea urchins in tide pools and on rocks or sand in shallow water.

## Atlantic Purple Sea Urchin

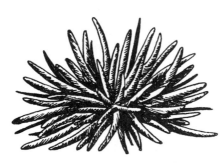 

*Color:* purple-brown
*Size:* 2 inches across, 3/4 inch high

The spines won't hurt you, so you can pick up sea urchins for a closer look. Careful, though! Like starfish, sea urchins have many tiny feet that could be hurt if you pick them up roughly. Sea urchins use their feet to gather food as well as to cling to rocks. Also like the starfish, the sea urchin's mouth is on the underside of its body, in the center.

Sea urchins like to hide, so you might have to turn over a rock or lift a clump of seaweed to find one. If you move a rock, do it slowly and carefully so you

# Green Sea Urchin

*Color:* green
*Size:* 3 1/4 inches across,
1 1/2 inches high

won't crush sea urchins and other animals that might
be hiding underneath. The shells of dead sea urchins
are very pretty and easy to find on many beaches. Look
for the illustration of an empty sea urchin shell in the
next chapter on page 48.

## Sand Dollar

Sand dollars are beautiful animals. They are flat and round like a cookie, with a five-point star design on top. Living sand dollars are covered with short spines. If you pick up a sand dollar and turn it upside down, you will see a small hole in the center. That is its mouth. Sand dollars may be found in tide pools, on the beach, or on Turtle Grass beds.

# Common Sand Dollar

*Color:* light brown
*Size:* 3 inches across

The **Common Sand Dollar** has a fancy design on top. All the lines and shapes in the design are in groups of five. Look for ten rows (five pairs) of ovals shaped like kernels of corn. There are five "kernels" in each row. In between each pair of kernel rows is a pair of triangles.

# Keyhole Urchin

*Color:* tan or gray
*Size:* 5 1/2 inches across

The **Keyhole Urchin** is a kind of sand dollar. It is larger and not as perfectly round as the Common Sand Dollar. Young Keyhole Urchins have five long, narrow slots in their bodies. Each slot is shaped like the keyhole of a door, which is how this animal got its name. The slots gradually fill in as the animal grows. The **Six-holed Keyhole Urchin** can bury itself in the sand in just a few minutes by turning its body from side to side.

# Six-holed Keyhole Urchin

*Color:* gray, tan, or light brown
*Size:* 4 1/2 inches across

### American Lobster

Two hundred years ago, there were so many lobsters that enough could be caught for a meal in a few minutes, using a net or, if careful, bare hands. Today, lobsters are still a popular food, but after many years of lobster fishing, they are much harder to find. Traps are used to catch them. The **American Lobster** lives both in the shallow, calm waters of coves and inlets and in deep water far out in the ocean.

The lobster has a hard shell on the outside and no skeleton on the inside. As it grows, it sheds its old shell after a new one has grown underneath. This is called *molting.* With their dark green coloring, lobsters can hide easily among rocks or seaweed. (Once in a while people find lobsters that are blue, yellow-green, or even white.)

Lobsters have a trick to help them escape from their enemies. If a big fish grabs the lobster's claw, the

## American Lobster

*Color:* dark green, sometimes blue or yellow-green
*Size:* 3 feet long

lobster can drop the claw from its body and swim away. Then the lobster grows a new claw in its place. It can also grow a new leg or antenna if one breaks off.

You probably won't see a live lobster among the rocks. (If you do, don't try to catch it. The lobster's claw is strong enough to break your finger, and the edges of its tail are very sharp.) Along the shore, you are more likely to find pieces of a lobster shell, left after a gull's meal or an outdoor lobster bake. The dark green shell will have turned red from baking in the sun or over a fire.

## Crab

There are many different types of crabs that live along the Atlantic coast. While you're looking for animals in the rocks and seaweed, you're almost sure to find a crab. But you will have to look closely. Like some other animals in the sea and on land, the crab can be hard to see because its coloring helps it blend in with its surroundings. This coloring, which is called *camouflage*, helps to protect the animal from its enemies.

Crabs move sideways, using the claws and feet on one side of the body to push and those on the other to pull. Crabs move very fast when they sense danger, so you might not see one close up unless it's dead. If you're quick enough to catch a crab, hold it from the back as you would a turtle, so that it can't pinch you with its claws, or *pincers*. A small crab can't harm you, but even a little pinch from a tiny claw could startle you. Dropping the crab might hurt it or even kill it.

The colors listed for each crab show the color of the top of the crab's shell.

# Lady Crab

*Color:* gray or tan with
dark purple spots
*Size:* 3 inches wide, 2 1/2
inches long

The **Lady Crab** looks like it has the measles; its
shell is covered with spots. Wait for low tide and look
for this crab along the water's edge. *But don't try to
pick up a Lady Crab.* They are not shy like most crabs
and they have long pincers that are very sharp.

# Atlantic Rock Crab

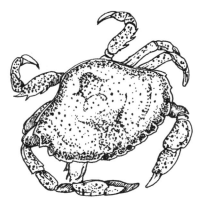

*Color:* yellow with many red
spots
*Size:* 5 1/4 inches wide, 3 1/2
inches long

The **Atlantic Rock Crab** is also spotted, but its
spots are red and its legs and short, fat pincers are
bright orange. The Atlantic Rock Crab lives along the
low-tide line. This crab is a popular seafood.

# Common Spider Crab

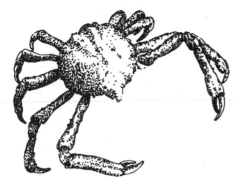

*Color:* gray or brown
*Size:* $3^3/_4$ inches wide,
4 inches long

The **Common Spider Crab** is easy to identify. All crabs have eight legs but the Spider Crab is the only crab that looks just like a big, fat spider. It lives along the low-tide line.

# Jonah Crab

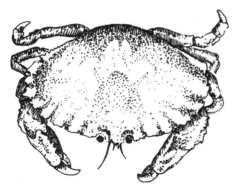

*Color:* brick red
*Size:* $6^1/_4$ inches wide,
4 inches long

The **Jonah Crab** is about the same size as the Atlantic Rock Crab, and its claws look the same. But the Jonah Crab's shell is oval and is the color of red brick. This crab lives in rocks and seaweed.

# Sand Fiddler Crab

*Color:* purple or gray-blue with darker markings; purple patch on top near front

*Size:* 1 1/2 inches wide; 1 inch long

You need a good imagination to see how fiddler crabs got their name. On a fiddler crab, one pincer is much larger than the other. The large pincer looks a little bit like a person's arm when it's playing a fiddle: bent at the elbow and holding a bow. The large pincer is covered with light-colored spots. The **Sand Fiddler Crab** is a kind of fiddler crab that lives in sandy and muddy places. Its black eyes are on top of the eyestalks that stick up from the top of its body.

The **Ghost Crab** makes its home in the sand right on the beach. The name tells about the way they look and the way they act. They are yellowish white—just the color of the sand in which they live—with white pincers. They run very fast, on their tiptoes, and they go in and out of the sand so quickly that they seem to disappear and reappear like magic. Their black eyes on long eyestalks stick up high from their bodies.

# Ghost Crab

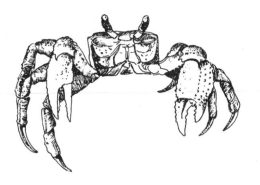

*Color:* light gray or yellow-white

*Size:* 2 inches wide, 1³/4 inches long

# Green Crab

*Color:* green with black markings

*Size:* 3 inches wide, 2¹/2 inches long

Tide pools are good places to look for **Green Crabs.** They are green and black on top and have large pincers that are both the same size. Green Crabs are especially common on the Maine coast.

# Blue Crab

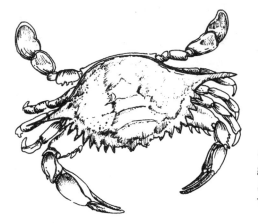

*Color:* blue-green or gray-blue

*Size:* 9 1/4 inches wide, 4 inches long

The **Blue Crab** has large, strong pincers and there are sharp points along the front edge of its body, so handle this crab carefully. The male has bright blue markings on its legs and pincers; the female has red markings. The Blue Crab is a popular seafood. You can see this crab near the low tide line. The Blue Crab is especially common in Chesapeake Bay.

The **Stone Crab** is also a popular seafood. It has larger pincers than any other crab on the Atlantic coast, and it has fat, hairy walking legs. You can find adults in the sand or mud near the low-tide line. Young Stone Crabs often live in Turtle Grass beds.

# Stone Crab

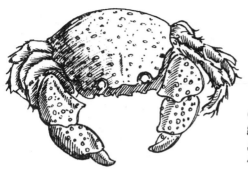

*Color:* dark red with gray spots

*Size:* 3 1/8 inches long, 4 5/8 inches wide

# Wharf Crab

*Color:* dark green or brown

*Size:* 3/4 inch long, 7/8 inch wide

**Wharf Crabs** are small but they are commonly seen because they are so friendly. They live among rocks, near docks and wharfs, and often climb into boats. If a Wharf Crab comes to visit you on a boat, it might be tempting to keep it for a pet. But, like all wild creatures, this little crab will be happier if you return it to its own environment, after exchanging a friendly *hello,* of course.

# Atlantic Mole Crab

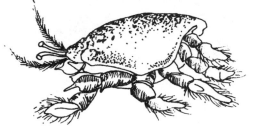

*Color:* light gray or tan
*Size:* 1 inch long, 3/4 inch wide

The best way to find an **Atlantic Mole Crab** is with your toes. They burrow in the wet sand and you can feel them when you walk along the edge of the water. You can also find them by digging in the wet sand. They can't hurt you because they don't have big claws as other crabs do. The Atlantic Mole Crab has a smooth body, shaped like a little barrel.

# Arrow Crab

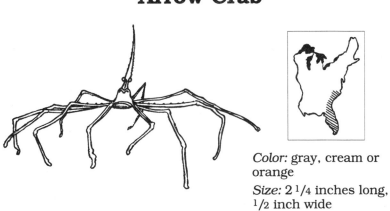

*Color:* gray, cream or orange
*Size:* 2 1/4 inches long, 1/2 inch wide

With its small body and long, spindly legs, the **Arrow Crab** looks more like its relative the spider. It is a small crab but easy to identify and, on some parts of the Florida coast, you can see dozens of them walking daintily along the Turtle Grass beds. They also can be found on rocks and wharf pilings. Named for its arrow-shaped head and V-shaped stripes, the Arrow Crab is a colorful animal with red legs, brighter red joints, blue pincers, and maroon eyes.

When you're looking for a **Hermit Crab**, don't look for a crab. Look for a snail shell. That's where a hermit crab lives. Unlike other crabs, a hermit crab has no shell of its own. It must use the empty shell of another animal for protection. If you see a snail shell moving fast instead of slowly, you can be sure there's a hermit crab inside.

Hermit crabs often can be found in tide pools and sometimes on the beach. When left on the beach by the tide, some sea animals dry out and die or are eaten by other animals. But the hermit crab just pulls far back into its shell and waits for the next high tide.

Like most other crabs, the hermit crab has two claws that it uses to catch its food and to protect itself. On a hermit crab, its right claw is always larger than its left. It uses its claws to pull its borrowed home along the rocks and sand. As the crab grows, it looks for a larger shell. Before moving in, the hermit crab pokes its claw inside the new shell to make sure the shell is empty. A hermit crab often shares its home with a small worm. The two animals help each other. The crab protects the worm and the worm keeps the inside of the shell clean by eating small bits of garbage.

# Long-clawed Hermit Crab

*Color:* gray or green-white
*Size:* 1/2 inch long, 3/8 inch wide

The **Long-clawed Hermit Crab** is the most common hermit crab on the Atlantic coast. This crab is so small that it can live in a periwinkle shell. The Long-clawed Hermit Crab has tan pincers. Some Long-clawed Hermits have a tan stripe on each pincer.

# Acadian Hermit Crab

*Color:* brown
*Size:* 1 1/4 inches long, 1 inch wide

The **Acadian Hermit Crab** is larger than the Long-clawed Hermit. It sometimes lives in a Moon Snail. Its pincers are also its front walking legs, and the right pincer-leg is much larger than the left. Its legs are orange or brownish red, and there is an orange stripe on the pincers. It has blue antennae and yellow eyes.

## Horseshoe Crab

The **Horseshoe Crab** is one of the oldest animals on earth. It lived with dinosaurs and looks the same today as it did then. One reason it has survived for so long is that it can live in waters that are very cold or very hot. It can even survive being frozen in ice. The Horseshoe Crab is related to crabs, but it is not really a crab. The Horseshoe Crab has body parts more like its closer relatives, the spider and the scorpion.

The Horseshoe Crab has a smooth, brown shell that is shaped like a horse's hoof. Along the bottom edge of the shell is a hard, horseshoe-shaped rim that it uses like a shovel to burrow into the sand or mud when it looks for worms and clams to eat.

It has a long, thin, strong tail that helps push the animal forward when it burrows. The tail also comes in handy when the Horseshoe Crab gets turned upside down. When you find a horseshoe crab, turn it gently over on its back. It is surprising how quickly the animal can flip itself over. While the Horseshoe Crab is upside down, get a quick look at its claws and its legs.

# Horseshoe Crab

*Color:* brown
*Size:* 2 feet long; 1 foot wide

A Horseshoe Crab has four eyes on top of its shell, and several light sensors underneath, but it cannot see very well. (It's not a very good swimmer, either.)

## Beach Flea

If you have ever been to an ocean beach, you probably have seen this annoying little creature. The beach flea is much larger than the flea you might find on your dog, but fortunately, it does not bite dogs *or* people. A beach flea is not an insect; it is related to crabs, shrimp, and lobster. Like the insect, however, the beach flea is a great jumper, which is why it is sometimes called a sand hopper. Beach fleas can swim, but they are most often seen in great numbers on piles of seaweed and other trash on the beach.

The **Big-eyed Beach Flea** is the most common beach flea on the Atlantic coast. As you might guess, it has very large eyes.

## Big-eyed Beach Flea

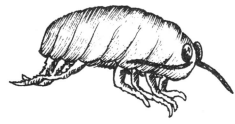 

*Color:* dark brown or gray
*Size:* 3/4 inch long

## Barnacle

This animal spends its whole adult life standing on its head. A barnacle begins life as a tiny worm called a larva. The larva floats in the water until it grows into an adult barnacle. Then it cements itself, head down, onto a rock, wharf, shell, or boat bottom. (The cement is limestone, which the barnacle makes from seawater.) The barnacle stays there for the rest of its life.

The barnacle eats by opening a tiny hole like a trapdoor at the top of its shell. It sticks out its tiny, feathery feet and kicks food into its mouth. You can watch a barnacle eat if you find one that is underwater. When the tide goes out, the barnacle closes the hole tightly to protect itself from the hot sun. Barnacles live together in large groups, called *colonies.*

# Large Rock Barnacle

*Color:* gray-white
*Size:* $3/4$ inch high,
$1 1/4$ inches wide

# Ivory Barnacle

*Color:* creamy white
*Size:* 1 inch high, 1 inch wide

# Bay Barnacle

*Color:* shiny white
*Size:* 1/4 inch high, 1/2 inch wide

# Little Gray Barnacle

*Color:* gray-white
*Size:* 1/4 inch high, 1/8 inch wide

# Northern Rock Barnacle

*Color:* white
*Size:* 1 inch high,
1/2 inch wide

## Limpet

The limpet is a small, cone-shaped animal that looks like a little hat. Some types of limpets have a small hole in the top of the cone. Its shell may be smooth or rough. Most limpets have brown and white stripes that run from the bottom of the shell to the top. A limpet makes its home by rubbing a shallow hole into a rock with its hard shell. The limpet can hold onto the rock so tightly that it can't be moved even by strong ocean waves. The limpet sometimes leaves its home at high tide, but it returns at low tide to eat.

The **Atlantic Plate Limpet** is a smooth shell that is sometimes called the "tortoise shell" limpet because of the pattern of its brown markings. The **Cayenne Keyhole Limpet** has a small hole at the top. It is not quite as rounded as the Atlantic Plate Limpet, and its shell has deep ridges that spread like rays from the top to the outer edge.

# Atlantic Plate Limpet

*Color:* white or tan with dark brown markings

*Size:* 7/8 to 1 3/4 inches long

# Cayenne Keyhole Limpet

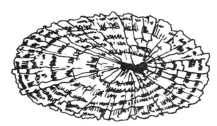

*Color:* dark gray or white with yellowish or light brown markings

*Size:* 5/8 to 1 3/4 inches long

## Snail

If you watch a snail move, you will see why snails are famous for being slow. A snail has only one foot. If you pick the snail up, you can see its head, with two antennae, and its foot (don't look for toes; the snail's foot is just a muscle). You have to be fast, because when the snail senses danger, it quickly pulls itself inside its shell. You might also try looking at the snail through a magnifying glass while it is moving. You might be able to see the tiny slit that is the snail's mouth. The snail also has a tongue and a row of sharp teeth, which are so small you need a microscope to see them.

Along the beaches and rocky shores of the Atlantic coast, you will see many different live snails and empty snail shells. You will also see snail trails—the line in the sand left by the snail's single flat foot. In the next chapter, you will find more illustrations of snails.

## Mussel

When you see a mussel at low tide, it's hard to believe it is alive. The two halves of its shell are closed, and it does not move at all. But when the tide comes in, the mussel opens its shell to let in seawater, which is filled with tiny plants and animals that mussels eat. Usually mussels wait for their food to be washed in with the waves, but a mussel can move slowly with its one foot if it needs to find food or protection.

You can find groups of mussels attached to the rocks or lying on the muddy bottoms of coves and saltwater rivers. The mussel attaches itself to rocks

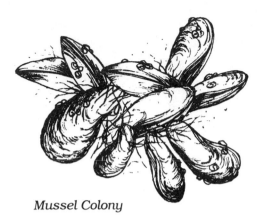

*Mussel Colony*

(and to other mussels) with strong, thin, brown threads that it makes with a gland in its foot. A group of mussels attached in this way is called a *bed*, or a *colony*, of mussels. Look for more illustrations of mussels in the next chapter, on pages 75–76.

## Chiton

It's hard to tell if this small animal is coming or going. It is a small oval that is shaped a lot like a turtle. If you look at an upside-down chiton, you might be able to see its foot and head, which are close together on one end. The chiton can't move fast, but its foot is very strong. You will find out how strong it is if you try to take a chiton off the rock or shell on which it lives. If you do get it off, it will quickly curl into a ball to protect itself. The **Common Eastern Chiton** is often found on slipper shells. The **Red Northern Chiton** can be found on rocks at low tide.

# Common Eastern Chiton

*Color:* light brown or dirty white

*Size:* $3/8$ to $3/4$ inch long

# Red Northern Chiton

*Color:* light yellow with red markings

*Size:* $1/2$ to 1 inch long

## Jellyfish

One good reason to wear shoes while you're exploring the shore is to protect your feet from jellyfish. If you touch a jellyfish, even if it is dead, you will be stung. A jellyfish doesn't sting like a bee. The animal is covered with tiny stingers that shoot poison "darts" when touched. These darts are so small that you need a microscope to see them. Some jellyfish stings make your skin itch for a few hours. Others can cause painful blisters. Some can kill you. *To be safe, never touch any jellyfish.*

As it floats near the surface of the ocean, a jellyfish uses its darts to kill small sea animals for food. A jellyfish is not really a fish; it has no scales, or fins, or gills. It feels and looks like jelly. The jellyfish is made mostly of water, and most of its body is a stomach. It is not a good swimmer, but it can move through the water by opening and closing its body, like an umbrella.

The **Moon Jellyfish,** the **Sea Nettle,** and the **Lion's Mane Jellyfish** are often washed up on beaches along the Atlantic coast. The **Upside-down Jellyfish** sometimes can be seen by the dozens or even the hundreds floating in shallow lagoons along the coast of Florida. This jellyfish is named for its habit of turning upside down when it sinks to the ocean floor to eat tiny animals that live there. The **Jellyball** or **Cannonball Jellyfish** is named for its round shape.

The **Moon Jellyfish** is mostly white and clear, like water. You can see colored body parts—yellow, brown, and pink—inside. It has many short tentacles.

## Moon Jellyfish

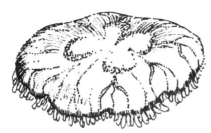

*Color:* white and clear
*Size:* 16 inches across

# Sea Nettle

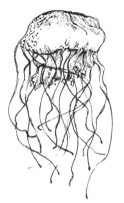

*Color:* pink with red stripes or white

*Size:* 10 inches across (pink) or 4 inches across (white)

There are two different kinds of **Sea Nettle.** One is pink with red stripes; the other is white. The pink Sea Nettle has forty tentacles; the white one is smaller and has twenty-four tentacles. Sea Nettles are especially common in Chesapeake Bay.

# Lion's Mane Jellyfish

*Color:* changes with age (see above)

*Size:* 8 feet across

The **Lion's Mane Jellyfish** is the largest jellyfish in the world. It can grow to be eight feet wide and has 150 tentacles. The Lion's Mane Jellyfish changes color as it grows. Young Lion's Mane Jellyfish (up to six inches) are pink or yellow; those from six to eighteen inches are red or dark yellow; larger ones are dark red or brown. *The Lion's Mane Jellyfish is very poisonous.*

# Upside-down Jellyfish

*Color:* dark green or muddy yellow

*Size:* 12 inches across

The body of the **Upside-down Jellyfish** is shaped like a cookie. Its eight arms, which can be green or brown, look like small, leafy stalks of celery.

# Cannonball Jellyfish

*Color:* yellow or light blue

*Size:* 7 inches across

The round, fat **Cannonball Jellyfish** has sixteen short tentacles, forked like a slingshot.

# Sea Anemone

A sea anemone looks more like a plant than an animal. Its tentacles look like flower petals as they wave back and forth in the water catching small sea animals to eat. The sea anemone is related to the jellyfish. Like the jellyfish, the sea anemone's tentacles have stingers that help it catch food. (They aren't dangerous to people, but they hurt.) And the sea anemone's body is mostly stomach. But the sea anemone does not float in the water as the jellyfish does. It lives underwater and attaches itself to a rock or sometimes to the hard shell of another animal, such as a crab. Some sea anemones bury themselves in the sand or mud.

Sea anemones can be hard to see because they like to live in dark places, protected from the sunlight. Look closely along the shady side of a tide pool and be very quiet. When the sea anemone senses danger, it pulls its tentacles into its body. Then it looks like a small tree stump or a mushroom. You might be able to watch this happen. When you spot a sea anemone, stay very still for a few minutes. Then make waves in the water with your hand or a stick. The animal will quickly pull in its tentacles.

# Frilled Anemone

*Color:* brown with light-colored tentacles

*Size:* 18 inches high

# Ghost Anemone

*Color:* light yellow and clear

*Size:* 1 1/2 inches high

# Lined Anemone

*Color:* white or tan

*Size:* 1 3/8 inches high

# Striped Anemone

*Color:* brown or green with yellow or orange stripes
*Size:* 3/4 inch high

## Worm

If you move a large rock near the low-tide line or dig in wet sand, you're likely to see a sea worm wriggling out of sight. Worms that live along the seashore can sting or bite, so if you want to get a closer look, catch the worm in a bucket or wear rubber gloves to protect your hands before you pick one up. You will have to move quickly. Like the night crawlers that might live in your backyard, seashore worms can dig fast. You can also see sea worms in fishing tackle shops because they are used for bait.

# Leafy Paddle Worm

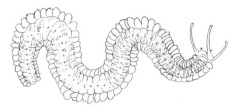

*Color:* gray, green, tan, or white
*Size:* 18 inches long

# Clam Worm

*Color:* shiny green or blue on top with tiny red, yellow, or white spots; reddish "paddles" all along its 200 segments
*Size:* 36 inches long

# Two-gilled Blood Worm

*Color:* pale pink
*Size:* 15 inches long

# Limulus Leech

*Color:* Cream or white
*Size:* $5/8$ inch long

This small creature is a good friend of the Horseshoe Crab. It attaches itself to legs and gills of the crab and feeds on tiny pieces of food it finds there. If the **Limulus Leech** is removed from the Horseshoe Crab, it will not eat and it begins to shrink.

# Sponge

For many years, experts couldn't decide whether the sponge was a plant or an animal. But finally it was decided that sponges are animals because they "catch" their food, by taking water into the tiny holes that cover their bodies. Plants make their own food.

What you see when you look at a sponge is its skeleton. Sponges use the holes that cover them for breathing as well as for collecting food. Some living sponges are covered with sharp, little needles, but these are too small to see without a microscope.

Even experts have trouble identifying different sponges because each kind can have many shapes, colors, and sizes. You might see living sponges attached to rocks or shells in tide pools or in shallow, protected places along the shore. You can often find pieces of dead sponges washed up on the beach.

As you can probably guess, the **Crumb-of-Bread Sponge** looks something like a piece of bread—not a slice, but a clump torn from a whole loaf. The **Finger Sponge** has many long branches that look like fingers. It is tan or pink, but if you find a piece on the beach it might be white, bleached by the sun. The **Red Beard Sponge** has fuzzy, red-orange branches.

# Crumb-of-Bread Sponge

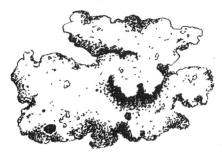

*Color:* tan or light yellow

*Size:* varies, usually found on the beach in clumps that will fit in your hand

# Finger Sponge

*Color:* tan or pink

*Size:* grows to 18 inches high

# Red Beard Sponge

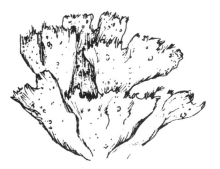

*Color:* red or orange

*Size:* varies from very thin layer to 8 inches thick

# 3. Shells to Collect

When you are exploring the shore, you might see the shells of some of the animals described in chapter 2. You will also find the shells of other sea creatures washed up on the beach or rocks. All the shells described in this chapter are mollusks, except for the sand dollar and the sea urchin.

A mollusk is an animal with a soft body that is protected by a hard shell. Some mollusks have one shell; some have two shells connected by a hinge. Many of the shells that you collect will be half of a two-shelled mollusk. But sometimes you can find an empty two-shelled mollusk that is still connected at the hinge.

On the inside of a two-shelled mollusk shell, you can usually see the place where the animal's foot, or muscle, was attached. Sometimes the spot is a darker color than the rest of the inside of the shell. This spot is called a muscle scar. Sometimes the color of the muscle scar can help you identify the shell.

*One-shelled mollusk
with growth lines*

*Two-shelled mollusk with
growth lines*

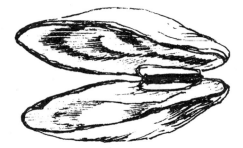

*Mollusk with hinge*

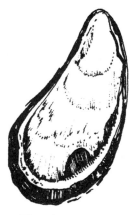

*Mollusk with skin*

*Muscle scar*

You can see how a mollusk has grown by its growth lines. On both one- and two-shelled mollusks, these growth lines curve together all around the shell. Sometimes these growth lines are flat, and sometimes they are ridges that you can see and feel easily.

Some mollusk shells, such as mussels or clams, are partly covered with a brown or black "skin." This skin protects the animal's shell from dissolving in the seawater. The "skin" is soft when the animal is in the water. It becomes dry and feels like thin paper after the empty shell has been on the rocks or sand for a while.

The size given with each shell description is the average size of a full-grown animal. You will find many shells that are smaller, and perhaps a few that are larger, than the sizes shown in this guidebook.

## Sand Dollar

You can find out about living sand dollars in chapter 2, "Sea Creatures." Like sea urchins, sand dollars lose their spines after they die. This shell is fragile, so carry it carefully.

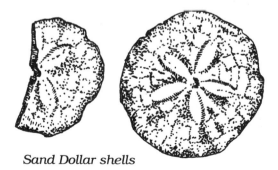

*Sand Dollar shells*

*Sea Urchin shells*

## Sea Urchin

You also can find out about living sea urchins in chapter 2, "Sea Creatures." The skeleton of a dead sea urchin is sometimes called the "jewel box of the sea" because of its beauty. You might find a dead sea urchin with all or most of its spines gone. You can see the many perfect rows of bumps where the spines were attached. Like sand dollars, their shells are fragile.

## Atlantic Dogwinkle

This is a common shell, but sometimes it is hard to identify because its color and shape are different, depending on what it eats and where it lives. Those that eat Blue Mussels have a dark shell—brown or reddish brown. Those that eat barnacles are lighter-colored—white, yellow, or light brown. The thick shell of the **Atlantic Dogwinkle** is covered with ridges. Atlantic Dogwinkles that live where the ocean has big waves have smaller ridges than those that live where the water is calm.

# Atlantic Dogwinkle

*Size:* 7/8 inch to 2 inches long

# Atlantic Oyster Drill

*Size:* 1/2 to 1 3/4 inches long

This shell is named for its favorite food—the oyster—and for the way it eats the oyster. It drills a hole in the oyster's shell and eats the soft body inside. The spiral-shaped shell is gray or brown and covered with thin ridges. You will find the **Atlantic Oyster Drill** wherever you find oysters. The Atlantic Oyster Drill also eats mussels and barnacles, so you might find one among the rocks or on a beach near rocks.

## Periwinkle

Periwinkles can live out of water for a longer time than many other sea creatures. The **Common Periwinkle** has a dark-colored shell—gray, brown, or black. It is very common among rocks and seaweed. The **Northern Yellow Periwinkle** is very small. It is light-colored—usually yellow, but sometimes white, orange, or tan. It has a smooth, shiny shell. Look for this periwinkle among rocks. The **Marsh Periwinkle** lives in salt marshes, but it is often found on beaches where it has been washed up by the waves. This periwinkle is white with brown spots.

# Common Periwinkle

*Size:* ⁵/8 to 1¹/2 inches long

# Marsh Periwinkle

*Size:* ³/4 to 1¹/4 inches long

# Northern Yellow Periwinkle

*Size:* ³/8 to ³/4 inch long

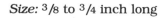

## Whelk

Of all the whelks described in this book, the **Eastern Mud Whelk** is the most common. It is also the smallest. This whelk is known by several different names, but part of its name is always mud: Common Mud Snail, Mud Dog Whelk, Eastern Mud Nassa, and Mud Basket. You may have guessed that the best place to look for this shell is in, or near, mud. The Eastern Mud Whelk has a thick spiral shell that is usually a dark color—brown, reddish brown, or almost black.

# Eastern Mud Whelk

Size: $5/8$ to $1 1/4$ inches long

# New England Basket Whelk

Size: $1/2$ to $7/8$ inch long

The **New England Basket Whelk** is another small whelk with several different names. It is sometimes called the New England Nassa, the New England Dog Whelk, or the Three-lined Basket Shell. Even though it has "New England" in its name, it is found all along the Atlantic coast, from Canada to Florida. It has a bumpy, spiral-shaped shell that is tan, yellowish-gray, or light orange. The New England Basket Whelk is found in sand or mud.

There are two large whelks commonly found on beaches from Cape Cod, Massachusetts, to Florida. They are the **Knobbed Whelk** and the **Channelled Whelk.** It is easy to tell these two whelks apart. The Channelled Whelk has a smooth shell that is tan or grayish on the outside and light pink on the inside. The Knobbed Whelk is tan with brown streaks on the outside and orange on the inside. It has rows of big bumps (knobs) on the fat part of the shell. Both of these whelks are found in sandy places.

The egg cases of these and other large whelks are fun to find on the beach. They look like necklaces: papery tan disks about the size of a quarter connected with a string. Sometimes the disks are filled with hundreds of tiny shells.

*Whelk egg case*

# Channelled Whelk

*Size:* 3 1/2 to 7 1/2 inches long

# Knobbed Whelk

*Size:* 4 to 9 inches long

# Shark Eye

*Size:* 7/8 to 3 inches long

The **Shark Eye** shell is smooth and shiny. It is white on the inside and gray, light brown, or light blue on the outside. On one side of the top is a beautiful swirl that looks like the number six (or the number nine). The middle of the swirl looks like an eye, which is how this shell got its name. Living Shark Eyes eat clams and other sea creatures that live in the sand, so you will probably find this shell on a sandy beach.

## Common Northern Moon Snail

*Size:* 1 1/2 to 5 inches long

This shell has an "eye" on one side of its outer shell, just as the Shark Eye does. But it is probably named for the half-moon-shaped opening of its shell. The **Common Northern Moon Snail** has a light gray or light yellow shell with darker-colored streaks. It is brown or tan on the inside. This shell is smooth, but not as shiny as the Shark Eye. The Common Northern Moon Snail can be found in the wet sand at low tide.

Slipper shells are often found attached to other shells, such as a mussel or a scallop or a Horseshoe Crab. You might also see slipper shells attached to each other in a pile. The top of the **Common Atlantic Slipper Shell** is rounded. It is white with many thin, brown lines. When you look at the inside of the shell, you will see how the slipper shell got its name. A thin "shelf" covers half of the shell, like the top of a slipper covers your foot.

# Common Atlantic Slipper Shell

*Size:* 3/4 to 2 1/2 inches long

# Cup-and-Saucer Shell

*Size:* 1 inch long

The **Cup-and-Saucer Shell,** like the limpet, looks like a pointed hat. The Cup-and-Saucer Shell is larger and more round on the bottom than the limpet. Living Cup-and-Saucers attach themselves to rocks, just as limpets do. But the easiest way to identify the Cup-and-Saucer Shell is by the small "cup" that is attached to the inside of the "saucer." The outside of the saucer is white or tan. The inside is brown and the cup is white.

# Common Jingle Shell

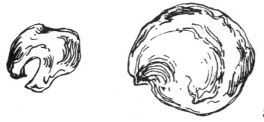 

*Size:* $3/4$ to $2\,1/4$ inches long

This shell is named for the sound that is made when several jingle shells are strung together to make a wind chime. Although these shells are so thin you can see through them, they are not too fragile. They feel and even look a little like a wrinkled toenail. The **Common Jingle Shell** is almost flat (except for its wrinkles) and is white, gray, or yellowish. Look for this shell on the beach.

# Bleeding Tooth

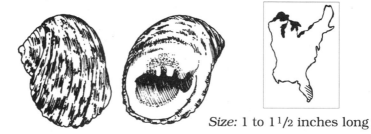

*Size:* 1 to $1\,1/2$ inches long

If you look inside the **Bleeding Tooth,** you can see how it got its name. There are several little white teeth surrounded by a red patch. The outside of its shell is dirty white with black and red marks. You can find them on the rocks of tidal pools.

# Common Dove Shell

*Size:* 3/8 to 7/8 inch long

Shell collectors and people who make jewelry with shells like the **Common Dove Shell** because of its colors and markings. It can be white with orange or yellow spots and lines or it can be brown with white markings. The shell is thick with many ridges on the outside. Look for a row of twelve white teeth along the lip.

# Florida Rock Shell

*Size:* 1 inch long

You can find this animal alive among the rocks at low tide. It is sometimes called a Florida Dye Shell because it can release colored liquid to hide from its enemies. The short, fat shell is gray with brown spots. It has four or five whorls.

# Scotch Bonnet

*Size:* 3 to 4 inches long

This shell is easy to identify. It is pale yellow or white with light brown squares in an even pattern. **Scotch Bonnets** can be smooth or have ridges on the outside. It is a thick shell with teeth along the lip. Look for these shells in shallow water or washed up on the beach.

# Common Purple Snail

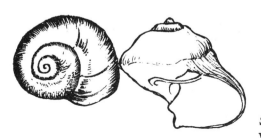

*Size:* 1 to 1 1/2 inches wide

This beautiful shell seems to glow with its shades of light and dark purple. It is a thin and delicate shell so it is difficult to find a whole, perfect one. The best time to look for the **Common Purple Snail** is after storms in the spring.

# Apple Murex

*Size:* 1/2 inch long

Look for the **Apple Murex** in shallow water. It doesn't feel or look like an apple. It is rough with deep ridges all around it. The outside is yellowish white with dark brown markings. Brown marks just inside the shell, near the lip, help identify the Apple Murex.

# Common American Sundial

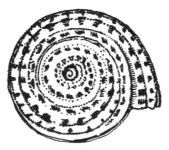

*Size:* 1 to 2 1/2 inches across

You probably can't tell time with this shell, but it will be a treasure in your shell collection. The top of the shell has a pattern of swirls and marks that make it look like a pinwheel. The bottom of the shell is flat. It is white or gray with brown or purple markings.

# West Indian Worm Shell

*Size:* 1 to 5 inches long

With its long body and cone-shaped end, this shell looks like a worm wearing a party hat. Young worm shells are tightly coiled, but older ones might have only two or three twists. They can be brown or pale yellow. Worm shells are often found near colonies of sponges.

# Angulate Wentletrap

*Size:* 1 inch long

There are many types of Wentletraps, but you can tell them apart if you examine them closely. They are sometimes called staircase shells because they look like a winding staircase. In fact, the name comes from the Dutch word *wenteltrap*, which means winding staircase. The **Angulate Wentletrap** is a shiny white with six or more whorls. Each whorl has nine or ten ribs. They are easy to find in the sand.

# Common American Auger

*Size:* 1 1/2 to 2 inches long

An auger is the name of a tool that carpenters use to drill holes. And that's what this shell looks like, a small drill. It is sometimes called the Little Screw Shell or the Atlantic Auger. The shell is light or dark gray, with darker bands of brown or dark purple. It has many whorls with twenty to twenty-five ribs on each whorl.

# Alphabet Cone

*Size:* 2 to 3 inches long

You might not find all the letters of the alphabet on this shell, but you can see some, if you use your imagination. The shell is smooth and creamy white with rows of brown and orange markings. It is shaped like a cone with a pointy top.

# Lettered Olive

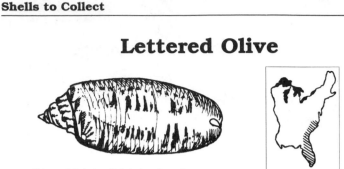

*Size:* 1³/₄ to 2³/₄ inches long

This shell is smooth like an olive with markings that look like the letters V or A. It is a slender shell with several "wrinkles" and creases. The **Lettered Olive** can be greenish gray or tan with dark brown markings.

# True Tulip

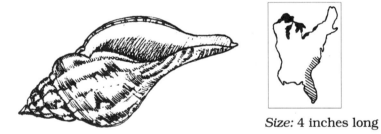

*Size:* 4 inches long

This shell doesn't look at all like a tulip, but the sack that it makes for its eggs does. You might find the flowerlike sack in shallow water in the mud or weeds. The shell of the **True Tulip** has many colors, but it is mostly white with brown marks. The inside is the color of cocoa.

# Florida Crown Conch

*Size:* 3 to 5 inches long

Conches are the shells that people like to put up to their ear and say they can hear the ocean roaring. **Florida Crown Conches** are usually found in coastal areas that are shaded by mango trees. There are many types of crown conches with different sizes, shapes, and colors. Many of them have a row of spines that stand straight up along the shell. The best way to identify a Florida Crown Conch is by the seven whorls at the top of the shell (sometimes called the spire). The shell is striped with shades of gray, brown, and pale yellow.

# Pink Conch

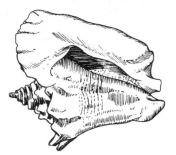 

*Size:* 10 inches long

The **Pink Conch** is sometimes called the Queen Conch. It is large and heavy and the inside of the lip is rosy pink. The outside is light yellow or brown. You can identify this shell by its size. Also, look for the side of the shell that sticks out like an open door.

# Coquina

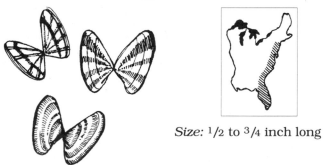

*Size:* 1/2 to 3/4 inch long

These tiny shells come in many colors—yellow, pink, purple, blue, red, or white, with patterns of darker colors like rays of sunshine. They look like jewels, and in some places on the coast of Florida there are so many it looks as if someone dumped out a treasure chest. They are sometimes called butterfly shells because the shape of the shell, opened and lying flat, looks like a butterfly.

# Sunray Venus

*Size:* 3 to 6 inches long

Venus clams are named for the Greek goddess Venus, who was graceful and beautiful. There are many of these shells in some places on the southern coast, especially in northwestern Florida. It is a smooth shell, pinkish gray on the outside with lines of purple spreading from the hinge like sunrays through a cloud. The inside is white.

# Turkey Wing

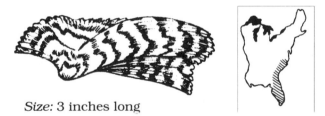

*Size:* 3 inches long

The **Turkey Wing** is a type of clam shell. It has two other names, **Noah's Ark** and **Zebra Ark.** All of these names describe it well. The shell looks like a boat when the animal is alive and attached to a rock. Each of the two shells is shaped like a turkey wing, and it is decorated with reddish-brown stripes that look like a zebra. The inside of the shell is pale purple with many marks that look like teeth.

# Angel Wing

*Size:* 8 inches long

## Angel Wing

If you find both halves of an angel wing's shell, you can easily see how this shell got its name. When the shell is opened flat, it looks like a pair of angel wings. The **False Angel Wing** and its close cousin, called simply the **Angel Wing,** or sometimes the **Fallen Angel Wing,** are similar in shape. But the False Angel Wing is much smaller. Both are beautiful, thin, white shells. They are long and narrow with ribs that run from the hinge to the outer edge of the shell. The ribs are bigger on an Angel Wing than on a False Angel Wing. Both live in mud.

# False Angel Wing

*Size:* 2 inches long

# Blood Ark

*Size:* 1 1/8 to 3 inches long

This shell is called a **Blood Ark** because, unlike other mollusks, it has red blood. Its shell is thick, with twenty-six or more wide ribs. It is white, but may have a fuzzy, brown covering on the outside. It lives in the sand or mud.

# Ponderous Ark

*Size:* 2 inches long

When the **Ponderous Ark** is alive it has a velvety dark covering on the outside. When it is not alive, the sturdy, round shell is mostly white. You can count between twenty-seven and thirty-one ribs on the outside. Inside, there are many little dents that look like teeth.

## Cockle Shell

Cockles are thick and rounded shells. Two small cockles are found along the Atlantic coast from Maine to North Carolina. They are called **Morton's Cockle** and the **Northern Dwarf Cockle.** Morton's Cockle is tan or white with brown, zigzag stripes. The Northern Dwarf Cockle is white with tan markings. It has wide ribs running from the hinge to the outside edge of the shell.

# Morton's Cockle

*Size:* ⁷/₈ inch across

# Northern Dwarf Cockle

*Size:* ¹/₂ inch across

# Strawberry Cockle

*Size:* 1 to 3 inches across

# Yellow Cockle

*Size:* 2 inches across

The **Strawberry Cockle** is cream-colored with speckles of reddish brown. It has thirty-three to thirty-six ridges running from the outer edge to the hinge of the shell. **Yellow Cockles** are usually yellow inside and out; they have thirty to forty ridges.

# Giant Atlantic Cockle

*Size:* 2 1/4 to 5 1/4 inches across

The **Giant Atlantic Cockle** is the largest cockle on the Atlantic coast; it lives farther south than the Morton's and Northern Dwarf cockles. It is tan or yellow with brown markings on the outside and pink or yellow on the inside. It has thick ribs as the Northern Dwarf Cockle does.

# Northern Cardita

*Size:* 1 1/2 inches long

This is a small, but thick, shell with about twenty "ribs" on the outside. It is white and smooth on the inside and brown on the outside. It lives in sand or mud.

# Atlantic Nut Clam

*Size:* 1/2 inch long

This tiny clam is shaped like a triangle. It is shiny white, like a pearl, on the inside and white with brownish green "skin" on the outside. Look for this shell in the sand or mud.

# File Yoldia

*Size:* 2 to 2 1/2 inches long

This is a delicate and fancy clam shell. It is green on the outside and bluish white on the inside. Along the hinge side of the shell, the edge is rough, like a file. One end of the shell is rounded, the other is slightly pointed.

# Atlantic Jackknife Clam

*Size:* 3 to 8 inches long

# Atlantic Razor Clam

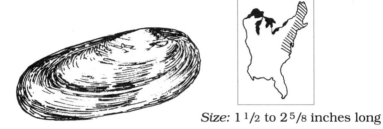

*Size:* 1 1/2 to 2 5/8 inches long

The **Atlantic Jackknife Clam** and **Atlantic Razor Clam** are named for their shapes and their sharp edges. (They are not sharp enough to cut you.) Both shells are shiny and greenish on the outside and white on the inside. The Razor Clam is round on the ends, and the Jackknife Clam looks more like a rectangle. Both shells are thin and fragile. You should carry the shells of these two animals carefully, so that they will not break.

The **Atlantic Surf Clam** is the largest clam on the east coast. Starfish and other sea creatures like to eat this clam, but it can sometimes jump to safety by using its big, strong foot. People like to eat this clam, too. The

# Atlantic Surf Clam

*Size:* 6 inches long

Atlantic Surf Clam is mostly white, with some yellow on the outside. It is shaped like a triangle with rounded points. This clam lives in the surf, where the waves break against the shore. It is found along many Atlantic coast beaches. This clam has several names. In Maine, for instance, it is sometimes called the Hen Clam. In some other places, it is known as the Beach Clam.

Here is another favorite eating clam. In fact, it is often called the Steamer Clam because of the way it is cooked. This clam lives in the mud. You may see a living **Soft-Shell Clam** squirt water up through the mud at low tide. If you see some holes in the mud or wet sand, look for some empty shells nearby. The Soft-Shell Clam is smaller, longer, and not as wide as the Atlantic Surf Clam. It is white, like chalk, inside and out.

# Soft-Shell Clam

*Size:* 3 inches long

## Quahog

The **Northern Quahog** (pronounced KO-hog) has many different names: Hard-shell Clam, Cherrystone Clam, and Littleneck. Indians made the shell of the quahog into tools and jewelry. They also used pieces of this shell, which they called *wampum,* for money, to trade for things that they wanted.

On some parts of the coast, people like to eat quahogs. Adult quahogs are about half the size of an adult Atlantic Surf Clam. The Northern Quahog is grayish yellow on the outside and white and shiny inside. Sometimes there is a light purple muscle scar on the inside. The **Ocean Quahog** is more rounded than the Northern Quahog and its shell is thicker. It is white inside and out but might be covered with a thin, black "skin". (See the introduction to this chapter, pages 45–47.)

# Northern Quahog

*Size:* 2 3/4 to 4 1/4 inches across

# Ocean Quahog

*Size:* 3 to 5 inches across

## Mussel

In chapter 2, "Sea Creatures," you can find out about living mussels. The **Northern Horse Mussel** has a large, oval shell. It is light purple on the outside but is usually covered with brown "skin"; it is gray on the inside. You can see curved growth rings on the outside of this shell.

# Northern Horse Mussel

*Size:* 2 to 9 inches long

The **Blue Mussel** has a thinner shell than the Northern Horse Mussel. It is light blue on the inside and gray on the outside, with a dark blue "skin." It has growth lines like the Northern Horse Mussel. In some places, the Blue Mussel is a popular seafood.

# Blue Mussel

*Size:* 1 1/4 to 4 inches long

# Atlantic Ribbed Mussel

*Size:* 2 to 5 inches long

The **Atlantic Ribbed Mussel** is easy to identify because of the ribs on its shell that run from the hinge to the outer edge. It is grayish-white on the outside, with brown "skin," and light blue on the inside.

# Eastern Oyster

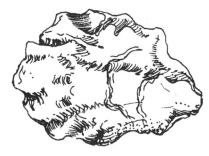

*Size:* 5 inches long

Oysters are like snowflakes; it's hard to find two exactly alike. Their shapes vary, depending upon where and how they live. Still, it is easy to identify an oyster because no other shell looks like it. The shell is very rough and bumpy on the outside and shiny smooth on the inside. Its color is dirty white or yellowish on the outside. Inside, there is a dark purple or black muscle scar where the body was attached. Oysters live in the shallow water of bays and saltwater rivers. Empty oyster shells are often found on the beach.

## Scallop

Scallops are a favorite seafood for many people, and they are popular with shell collectors because of their beautiful shells. A scallop shell is easy to identify. They are almost flat and mostly round, with a straight edge at the hinge. There are thin ribs running from the hinge to the outer edge. The **Atlantic Deep Sea Scallop** can be as big as a dinner plate. It is tan or brown on the outside. The **Atlantic Bay Scallop** is much smaller. It is gray, yellowish, or red-brown on the outside. Both scallops are white on the inside.

# Atlantic Deep Sea Scallop

*Size:* 8 inches long

# Atlantic Bay Scallop

*Size:* 3 inches long

### Pen Shell

These shells look more like fans than pens. They are nearly flat, wide at the top, and pointed at the opposite end. Some Pen Shells are orange; others are dark-colored, greenish brown. The **Stiff Pen Shell** has ridges that run along the length of the shell. The **Saw-toothed Pen Shell** is not quite as flat and is more smooth, with many fine ridges along the upper edge. Pen Shells are delicate and break easily so it might be difficult to find a whole one.

# Stiff Pen Shell

*Size:* 5 to 10 inches long

# Saw-toothed Pen Shell

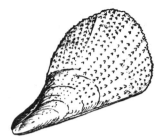 

*Size:* 6 to 12 inches long

# 4. Seashore Plants

## In the Sea

The ocean has beautiful gardens of plants, commonly called seaweed. Sea animals need seaweed, just as land animals need land plants. Seaweed provides food and shelter.

Land plants use roots to get food and water and stay in the soil. But seaweed does not have roots. Seaweed has a *holdfast,* which looks like a root. The holdfast keeps the seaweed attached to rocks or shells even when the sea is rough. If you try to pull the holdfast loose, you will see why it is called a holdfast.

There are many different types and colors of seaweed. Seaweed that lives near the surface of the water is green. Brown, red, and purple seaweeds are found in deeper, colder water. You can

*Holdfast*

see some seaweed growing along the water's edge, but many kinds are left on the beach by the tide, especially after a storm. Some seaweeds are good to eat, but check with an adult before sampling any wild-growing plant.

# Green Thread Algae

*Color:* bright green
*Size:* 1/4 inch thick, 2 feet long

*Alga* is the Latin word for seaweed, which makes sense because all seaweeds are algae. Algae are simple plants that have no stems or roots. Most algae live in water. **Green Thread Algae** grows in tide pools and in salt marshes. You also might see it on boat docks and buoys. In Florida it grows on the roots of mangrove trees. On the beach you might find it attached to shells or other debris that have been washed up by ocean waves. Green Thread Algae grows in big clumps, tangled up, and looks something like green spaghetti that has been cooked too long.

Low tide is the best time to get a close look at the brown seaweed known as **Rockweed.** It has many flat branches, each with a rib in the middle. The branches are covered with pairs of oval-shaped bumps. These bumps are called air bladders (Rockweed is sometimes called Bladder Wrack). The air bladders are like little water wings, which help the seaweed float on the

# Rockweed

*Color:* brown
*Size:* up to 3 feet

# Knotted Wrack

*Color:* brown
*Size:* up to 2 feet

surface of the water. This seaweed needs to stay on the surface to get sunlight. Like other plants, seaweed makes its own food from sunlight. Large beds of Rockweed cover the rocks in many places on the coast.

**Knotted Wrack** looks like its close relative, the **Knotted Rockweed.** The branches of Knotted Wrack, however, are thinner and have no rib in the center. The air bladders on the Knotted Wrack grow singly on the branches, rather than in pairs. In the winter, small, round, yellow, leaflike bumps grow along the branches. This seaweed is found in calm water and on rocks in salt marshes. Knotted Wrack is sometimes called Yellow Tang or Sea Whistle.

# Kelp

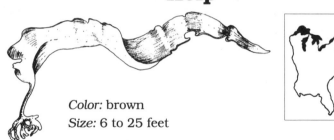

*Color:* brown
*Size:* 6 to 25 feet

With its long, flat, wide blade, **Kelp** is easy to identify. The blade has a long stem, like a tail, with a holdfast on the end. The stem can be as long as a room is tall. Kelp grows in mussel beds and under docks. When you find Kelp on the beach, the holdfast may still be attached to a mussel shell.

# Dulse

*Size:* 20 inches long

This large-leafed seaweed is a popular food in some places. It can be dried and added as a seasoning to soups and salad dressings, or it can be eaten in dried pieces that are something like potato chips. If you find a piece of **Dulse** growing among the rocks or lying on the beach, you might not think it looks or feels very tasty. It is brown or dark red and feels like leather. Dulse often grows on, or near, Kelp.

# Sea Colander

*Color:* brown
*Size:* 1 1/2 feet long

Here is another seaweed with a wide blade that is
found along the New England coast and farther north.
But this one is full of holes. That is why it is called a
*colander* (a colander is a pot with holes that is used to
drain water from spaghetti after it is cooked). The
brown blade of the **Sea Colander** has a thick rib in the
middle. The blade of the Sea Colander is shorter and
wider than a Kelp blade, and the stem is much shorter.
The Sea Colander is sometimes called Devil's Apron.

Also called Green Laver, **Sea Lettuce** looks like
other lettuce. It has flat, thin, green leaves that are
wavy on the edges. These leaves can grow to be two
feet long, but the leaves are so thin and delicate that
you usually find much smaller pieces of it on the
beach. You may see it growing in quiet coves and salt
marshes all along the Atlantic coast. Like other lettuce,
Sea Lettuce can be eaten.

# Sea Lettuce

*Color:* green
*Size:* 1 to 2 feet long

# Purple Laver

*Color:* purple, pink, red, or brown
*Size:* 6 inches long

**Purple Laver** is a popular food in some places, especially Japan, where it is wrapped around rice or fish, put in soup, or eaten by itself. As you might guess, Purple Laver is closely related to Green Laver, but it is, of course, a different color. Although it is called purple, it may be pink, reddish, or brownish. Like Green Laver, it has flat, thin leaves that are wavy on the edges. It grows where the water is calm, in large beds, or colonies, attached to rocks or other seaweeds.

# Sea Grass

*Color:* green
*Size:* up to 6 feet tall

This seaweed looks like grass that needs to be ironed. It has long wrinkled green blades that may be a foot or more tall. **Sea Grass,** sometimes called Maiden Hair, grows on rocks all along the coast from Canada to South Carolina. Another kind of sea grass, called **Link Confetti,** can be found as far south as Florida. It is bright green and its hollow blades have air bubbles that look like bumps. Link Confetti sea grass is taller than its cousin, the Sea Grass, and it can grow where the water is muddy and dirty.

# Link Confetti

*Color:* green
*Size:* 2 to 3 feet

# Irish Moss

*Color:* purple, red, reddish green, or yellowish white

*Size:* 2 to 4 inches high

This seaweed is called **Irish Moss** because it also grows in Ireland. There it was used for cooking and medicine long before Columbus discovered America. It is also eaten in New England, where it is found all along the coast. Many New England cookbooks have a recipe for pudding made with Irish Moss. This plant is small, with many flat branches.

# Chenille Weed

*Color:* bright red

*Size:* up to 2 feet tall

This is a beautiful red plant with many branches. The branches and stem are covered with soft leaves that look like hair. It grows underwater in protected places on the Atlantic coast.

# Sea Potato

*Color:* dark green or
yellowish brown
*Size:* 1 to 3 inches long

The **Sea Potato** looks more like cauliflower than a
potato. It also looks a little like a brain, which is why it
is sometimes called Rat's Brain. It grows in clumps
that feel like a sponge. The clumps are hollow inside.
Because it is hollow, it floats in the water. The Sea
Potato is often found attached to Irish Moss or another
seaweed.

## Near the Sea

Only special plants can live in the salty air of the
seashore. The many flowers, plants, and grasses that
decorate the Atlantic coast must be able to live in cold
and hot weather and to survive ocean storms and high
winds. The grasses of the seashore are a pretty sight
along salt marshes and beaches. But they are much
more than that. On beaches and dunes, grasses keep
the sand from blowing away. In the salt marsh, grasses
make safe nesting and feeding places for many birds
and other creatures. When you explore the dunes, be
careful not to walk on the fragile grasses, and stay on
paths or walkways.

# Eelgrass

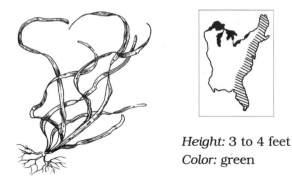

*Height:* 3 to 4 feet
*Color:* green

This grass lives in salt water, but it is not a seaweed. Its roots are buried in the sand or mud beneath the water. You can see its long, flat, green leaves, waving like ribbons near the surface of shallow coves and rivers, all along the Atlantic coast. **Eelgrass** makes a good hiding place for crabs, fishes, and other sea creatures.

# Turtle Grass

*Height:* 1 foot
*Color:* green

Like Eelgrass, **Turtle Grass** grows underwater. It looks similar but its blades are wider than Eelgrass blades. Also, Turtle Grass lives where the ocean is warmer, in the Florida Keys and on the Gulf of Florida. Turtle Grass and Eelgrass never grow in the same place. Many sea creatures make their home in Turtle Grass.

# American Beach Grass

*Height:* 2 to 4 feet
*Color:* green

This is the most common plant on the beaches and dunes of the Atlantic coast. It is also one of the most important. Its strong, deep roots connect under the sand, helping to keep the sand from blowing away. **American Beach Grass** is tall, and its stem is strong and flat.

# Sea Oats

*Height:* 3 to 6 feet
*Color:* green

From Virginia to Florida, **Sea Oats** grows on the dunes with American Beach Grass. Sea Oats is a taller plant, and it has large flower clusters at the top that look like the tail feathers of an ostrich.

# Reed Grass

*Height:* 10 to 12 feet
*Color:* green

This is the tallest grass on the Atlantic coast. It stands ten or twelve feet tall and grows in large colonies in salt marshes. Walking or riding past a salt marsh, you can see the fat cluster of seeds at the top of the **Reed Grass,** and you can hear the soft rustling sound the Reed Grass makes when the wind blows.

# Saltmarsh Bullrush

*Height:* 4 to 6 feet

You may see this plant near some Reed Grass. It is shorter than Reed Grass and it has long, sharp leaves. In the summer and fall, you can see brown, oval seeds in bunches where the leaf grows out of the stem.

# Saltmarsh Cordgrass

*Height:* 2 to 8 feet

Although their names are similar, this cordgrass looks different from **Saltmeadow Cordgrass. Saltmarsh Cordgrass** is twice as tall, and it grows closely together in groups in the mud of marshes or saltwater riverbanks. It has wider leaves than Saltmeadow Cordgrass, and its flower is white.

You can see huge fields of Saltmeadow Cordgrass grass in salt marshes. It is easy to identify because it doesn't stand tall as other grasses do. It looks flattened, as if large animals have been lying on it. But it is really the wind that flattens Saltmeadow Cordgrass, which bends over easily because of its thin stem. It can grow to be three feet tall, but it is hard to tell its height since the grass is lying down. In late summer, Saltmeadow Cordgrass has purple flowers at the top of its blades.

# Saltmeadow Cordgrass

*Height:* 1 to 3 feet

# Spike Grass

*Height:* 1 to 2 feet

**Spike Grass** is a shorter grass that grows in higher spots in salt marshes. It has a tough stem with flat, pointed leaves. In late summer and early fall it has a light green cluster of flowers at the top of the stem.

A relative of the cactus, **Glasswort** is a tough little plant with a thick stem and many branches. These branches are green in the summer and bright red or brown in the fall. They look like many short pieces of branches hooked together like sausage links. This plant feels rubbery when you touch it. Like the cactus, Glasswort doesn't need much water, and it can store water in its branches. It grows in salty, sandy dirt near salt marshes and beaches.

# Glasswort

*Height:* 12 inches

# Sea Lavender

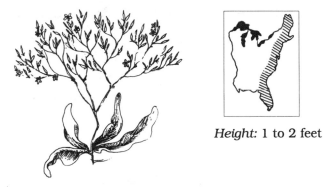

*Height:* 1 to 2 feet

**Sea Lavender** and Glasswort are often seen growing together along the edge of a salt marsh. Like Glasswort, Sea Lavender has many branches. The two plants are often the same height, although in some places, Sea Lavender can be two feet tall. And they are different in other ways. Sea Lavender is not related to cactus. In the summertime, many tiny, delicate, lavender flowers grow on the branches of the Sea Lavender, which is how this plant got its name. Sea Lavender has tiny, green leaves that are shaped like little spoons. There are several large leaves at the bottom of the plant.

# Sea Rocket

*Height:* 6 to 18 inches

In some places on the Atlantic coast, this is the only plant you will see growing right on the beach. **Sea Rocket** is tough enough to live in the salty sand, and its thick, rubbery leaves can hold water, just as the leaves of a cactus can. It also grows on dunes. Sea Rocket is named for the shape of the green seedpods that grow on the plant. In the summer, it has light blue or lavender flowers.

# Dusty Miller

*Height:* 2 feet

It's easy to identify this plant. The light green leaves of **Dusty Miller** are covered with tiny white hairs that make the plant look as if it is covered with dust. These little hairs help protect the plant from both hot sun and cold weather. Dusty Miller does not grow in bunches. You often see many single plants growing on the dunes and along the edge of a beach. In summer, Dusty Miller has a bright yellow flower. It blooms on top of a stalk that grows out of the top of the plant.

# Beach Heather

*Height:* 8 to 12 inches

This plant looks like a little bush. It is less than a foot tall and grows in groups along beaches and sand dunes. You can see from the little mounds of sand at the bottom of the plants that **Beach Heather** roots help hold the sand in place. Beach Heather has small, green, fuzzy leaves. For a short time in late spring or early summer, Beach Heather is covered with tiny, bright yellow flowers.

# Seaside Goldenrod

*Height:* 2 to 8 feet

This plant stands tall along the dunes and on the edges of salt marshes. It can be eight feet tall. Sometimes it is only two feet tall, but it is almost always taller than the other flowering plants growing around it. Often you see many **Seaside Goldenrod** plants growing together. They have long, pointed, green leaves. Seaside Goldenrod is easiest to identify from early summer to late fall, when clusters of golden yellow flowers grow on top of the stem.

## Beach Pea

*Height:* 2 to 3 feet

The **Beach Pea** looks a lot like the pea plant that grows in vegetable gardens. It grows a vine that crawls along the dunes. Green leaves grow in pairs from stems that are attached to the plant's main stem. The ends of the leaf stems curl like little pigs' tails. These curly little ends, called *tendrils,* wind around dune grasses and other plants. They help hold the plant in place. The Beach Pea has delicate pink or purple flowers all summer long. Its seedpods look like the seedpods of its cousin, the garden pea, and they are good to eat. Many birds and small animals, and some people, eat the seedpods.

# Beach Rose

*Height:* 3 to 6 feet

This wild rose has many names: Sea Rose, Salt-spray Rose, and Wrinkled Rose. It is a bush with many woody branches. You will often find many **Beach Rose** bushes growing together in thick hedges. These hedges are sometimes six feet tall. Beautiful pink and white flowers with yellow centers bloom on Beach Rose stems all summer long. Be careful if you pick one. The stems are covered with sharp thorns. In the fall and winter, the Beach Rose has round, red seedpods the size of a large marble. These seedpods are the fruit of the Beach Rose. They are called *rose hips.* They are good to eat. Sometimes people use them to make jelly or tea.

# Bayberry

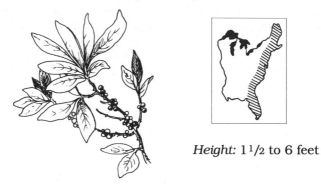

*Height:* 1 1/2 to 6 feet

Like the Beach Rose, **Bayberry** is a bush with woody stems. Its dark green leaves have a wonderful smell. You may have smelled Bayberry in your kitchen. It is used to flavor soups, spaghetti, and other foods. Bayberry has no flower that you can see, but in the summer and fall, it has bunches of grayish white berries growing on its stems. These berries are covered with wax and are not good to eat. From New Jersey to Florida, you might see a close relative of the Bayberry, called Wax Myrtle. The two plants look alike, but Wax Myrtle can be as tall as a tree.

## Mangrove Tree

These plants grow along the edge of ocean bays and swamps in Florida. They have shiny, leathery leaves. There are three different kinds of mangrove trees. They look similar but not exactly alike. The place they are growing can help you identify them. The **Red Mangrove** grows farthest out in the water. Its green, leathery leaves have black dots underneath. The flowers are pale yellow. The **Black Mangrove** grows

*Mangrove tree*

closer to shore, behind the Red Mangrove. Its leaves are fuzzy and the flowers are white. The **White Mangrove** also has white flowers, but its leaves are shiny and leathery. They live farthest back from the water, behind Black Mangroves.

# Red Mangrove

*Height:* 20 feet

# Black Mangrove

*Height:* 10 to 40 feet

# White Mangrove

*Height:* 20 to 40 feet

# 5. Insects

Most of the insects listed below are found inland as well as on the coast. Except for the grasshopper and the cricket, they are creatures to avoid because they bite or sting.

The **Eastern Sand Wasp** can be found throughout North America, but it is especially common on sand dunes and beaches. Its body is black with pale yellow stripes. It has bright yellow legs.

## Eastern Sand Wasp

*Size:* 1/2 inch long

# Deer Fly

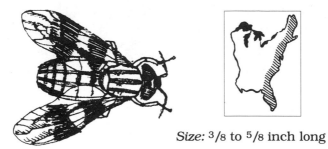

*Size:* 3/8 to 5/8 inch long

Deer flies like to bite deer, but they can be a real pest to people, too. They live in woodlands and meadows but are often seen along the seashore, especially if there are woods nearby. They give a painful bite as soon as they land on their victim. The body is black with light green markings. A deer fly is easy to recognize by its wings, which have black bands and make a triangle shape when it is not flying.

# American Horse Fly

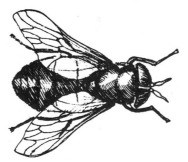 

*Size:* 3/4 to 1 inch long

The **American Horse Fly** is another insect with a mean bite. It is sometimes called a "Green Head" because of its large green eyes, which make this insect easy to identify. It is often seen on beaches and salt marshes.

# Saltmarsh Mosquito

*Size:* 1/8 to 1/4 inch long

**Saltmarsh Mosquitoes** are like all North American mosquitos except that they prefer to live near salt water. They can be golden brown or black.

## Tick

The tick that you might find on your dog or cat will sometimes bite people, but the bite, although it can hurt and itch, is not harmful to most people. There is a smaller tick, however, whose bite can cause a sickness called Lyme Disease. This tick has different names in different parts of the United States. It is sometimes called a deer tick, a bear tick, or a sheep tick.

The symptoms of Lyme Disease can include a rash, headache, sore or stiff muscles or joints, a fever, swollen glands, or red, itchy eyes. If the disease is not

# Dog Tick

*Color:* dark brown
*Size:* 1/8 inch long

# Deer Tick

*Color:* dark brown
*Size:* 1/16 long

treated it can lead to more serious symptoms, such as heart problems or arthritis. Lyme Disease can be treated with antibiotics.

All ticks have eight legs, like a spider. Deer ticks are found in tall grass, bushes, and in the woods; along the seashore; and inland. To prevent being bitten by a tick, wear long pants tucked into your socks when you walk in the woods or in tall grass. Place a blanket or some other covering on the ground before sitting down.

# Seaside Grasshopper

*Color:* light brown or gray with small black spots; light yellow back wings
*Size:* 1 to 1 1/4 inches long

This insect is as likely to be found resting in the sand among the dunes as it is hopping in the grass. It has knobby knees and bulging eyes like the grasshoppers you probably see in your yard.

# Field Cricket

*Color:* black or dark brown
*Size:* 1/2 to 1 inch long

Another great hopper, this insect was made famous by Pinocchio's conscience, Jiminy Cricket. It is shaped much like a grasshopper, but smaller. A field cricket has a very big voice for its size. Listen for three loud chirps in the tall grass. If you live where it gets cold in the autumn, you will probably hear a cricket in your house. They come inside to get warm.

# 6. Shorebirds

At first, it might seem that identifying birds is a lot harder than identifying a shell in your hand or a plant that's growing in the ground. But each bird has its own color and shape and with a little practice, you will find that many birds are easy to identify, too. The pattern and coloring of a bird's feathers are called its *field marks*. The field marks to look for are included in the descriptions that follow. The size shown for each bird is the length of an adult bird from the tip of its bill to the tip of its tail.

The **Great Blue Heron** is easy to identify because it is so big. It is more than three feet tall, with wings that reach nearly seven feet from tip to tip. The Great Blue Heron is the largest shorebird on the Atlantic coast. Its body and wings are gray-blue; its head and the front of its long neck are mostly white. It has an orange bill and long yellow legs.

Look for this bird standing tall in marsh grass or at the edge of a quiet cove. When it's looking for food, the

# Great Blue Heron

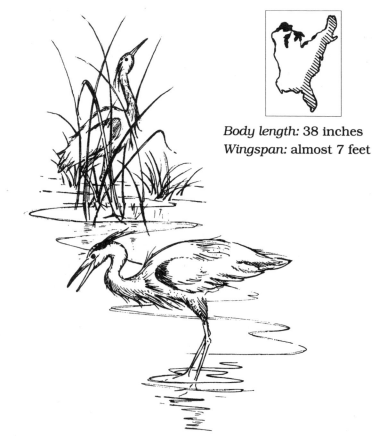

*Body length:* 38 inches
*Wingspan:* almost 7 feet

Great Blue Heron stands so still that it sometimes looks like a long stick poking out of the water. When it spots something to eat—a fish, shrimp, or bug—the bird's long neck snaps forward and the heron grabs its prey with its sharp beak. When it flies, the Great Blue Heron holds its neck in the shape of the letter **S** and lets its long legs trail behind. You might see Great Blue Herons in streams, rivers, ponds, and lakes, as well as along the coast.

# Great White Egret

*Body length:* 32 inches

*Wingspan:* 5 1/2 feet

Not long ago, egrets were hunted for their beautiful white feathers, which were used to decorate fancy hats. Now the birds are protected from hunters by law, and they can be seen in many places along the Atlantic coast. Egrets are members of the heron family. They like the same foods, and they hunt and live in the same places—shallow, marshy coves and inlets. The **Great White Egret** is smaller than its relative, the Great Blue Heron. Its feathers are pure white, its bill bright yellow, and its legs and feet shiny black.

# Snowy Egret

*Body length:* 20 inches
*Wingspan:* 3 feet

The **Snowy Egret** is all white, too. It is about half the size of a Great Blue Heron. It has a black bill, black legs, and bright yellow feet.

## Sandpiper

There are many kinds of sandpipers. Most sandpipers seen on the Atlantic coast have tan backs, white bellies, and dark spots on their breasts. Compared to other shorebirds, most sandpipers are small—about the size of a sparrow. Their legs are longer than a sparrow's though, and they have long, thin bills that they use to catch tiny sea creatures along the edge of the water. It's fun to watch them feed because they look like windup toys. They run so fast you can hardly see their legs. Their heads and tails bob up and down, and they all move together, like dancers on a stage.

# Least Sandpiper

*Body length:* 4 3/4 inches

Look for the **Least Sandpiper** along the muddy edges of rivers and salt marshes. It is brown on top and has a streaked breast and white belly. It has a dark brown bill, a white stripe above its eyes, and yellow legs. Even though it is called the Least Sandpiper, it is one of the most common sandpipers in the United States.

# Semipalmated Sandpiper

*Body length:* 5 inches

The **Semipalmated Sandpiper** is one of the most common shorebirds on the Atlantic coast. It looks like the Least Sandpiper, but its body is gray on top and it has black legs. It also has a black bill.

# Purple Sandpiper

*Body length:* 8 inches

The **Purple Sandpiper** is not really purple. Its back and breast are streaked dark gray and white. Its belly is white and it has yellow legs and a yellow bill with a black point. Purple Sandpipers are common in rocky places all along the Atlantic coast.

# Spotted Sandpiper

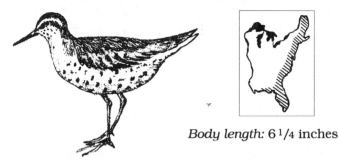

*Body length:* 6 1/4 inches

The **Spotted Sandpiper** is common all along the Atlantic coast. It has a brown back and brown wings. There is a white stripe above each eye. In summer, its white breast and belly are covered with dark spots. It has yellow legs and a yellow bill with a black point. This is one of the few sandpipers that is often seen by itself.

# Sanderlings

*Body length:* 6 1/2 inches

**Sanderlings** are often seen on sandy beaches at the edge of the water. This sandpiper has a white breast, a black bill, and black legs. In summer, its back and breast are tan with dark gray streaks; in winter its back is light gray with dark gray streaks.

## Tern

Terns are slender, fast-flying shorebirds. When looking for food, a tern flies with its sharp bill pointed down. If it sees a fish or bug in the water below, the tern dives straight down to snatch its prey from the water. There are several kinds of terns that you might see along the Atlantic coast. They look so much alike that even expert bird watchers sometimes have trouble telling them apart. They all have tails shaped like the letter V. They have white bodies; narrow gray wings; long, sharp bills; and black caps on their heads. They are all about the same size. But they are also different in some ways.

# Caspian Tern

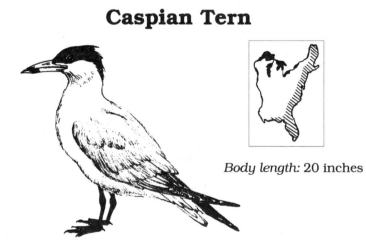

*Body length:* 20 inches

The **Caspian Tern** is the largest of the terns described in this book. It is shaped more like a gull than other terns, and it has a bright red bill and black feet.

# Common Tern

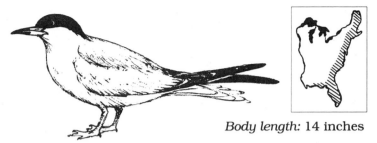

*Body length:* 14 inches

The **Common Tern**'s wings are longer than its tail. The tail is dark gray along the outside edge and the wings are dark gray on the tips. The Common Tern has a bright, red-orange bill (sometimes with a black tip) and feet the same color.

# Forster's Tern

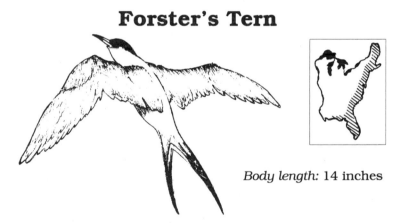

*Body length:* 14 inches

The **Forster's Tern** looks a lot like the Common Tern, but its tail is light gray with a darker gray band along the inside of the V. It has yellow-orange feet and a yellow-orange bill with a black point. The Forster's Tern is easiest to identify in the winter, when it has a narrow, black patch around its eyes. This tern is most often seen in salt marshes.

# Roseate Tern

*Body length:* 15 inches

The **Roseate Tern** has an all-white tail. Just the opposite of the Common Tern, the Roseate Tern's tail is longer than its wings. The Roseate Tern has a black bill and orange feet.

## Gull

The most common gulls along the Atlantic coast are the **Herring Gull,** the **Great Black-backed Gull,** and the **Laughing Gull.** Like other gulls, they are strong birds with long wings, webbed feet, and a strong, hooked bill. They will eat anything from fish that they catch in the water to peanut butter sandwiches and potato chips left by picnickers. They hang around anywhere they can grab a snack—the beach, a fish pier, even garbage dumps. Gulls have a trick for eating food that has a hard shell, like a crab or a clam. After the bird grabs its prey from the rocks or the sand, it flies up in the air and drops the prey on the rocks to break the shell. Then the gull can easily eat the soft meat inside. Gulls are most beautiful, though, when soaring like a glider on the ocean breeze.

The **Herring Gull** and the **Great Black-backed Gull** are often seen together. Both are snowy white, except for

118

their backs and the tops of their wings. They both have pale pink legs and a yellow bill with a red spot on the bottom. But it is easy to tell them apart. The Herring Gull has a gray back and gray wings with black tips. The Great Black-backed Gull has a black back and wings and is larger than the Herring Gull. When these two birds have an argument, the Great Black-backed Gull always wins!

If you see many of these gulls together, you may see some gull-sized birds that are the color of mud. These are not different kinds of gulls. They are just young Herring or Great Black-backed gulls. Like some other gulls, these birds do not get their full adult colors until they are two or three years old.

# Herring Gull

*Body length:* 20 inches

# Great Black-backed Gull

*Body length:* 2 feet

# Laughing Gull

*Body length:* 1 foot

You can identify the **Laughing Gull** with your eyes closed. Its loud ha-ha-ha-ha-ha can be heard all along the Atlantic coast. But even when the Laughing Gull is not "laughing," it is easy to identify. It has a black head; a white rim around its eyes; and a snow-white breast, neck, and belly. Its bill and feet are dark orange. The Laughing Gull has a gray back and wings, but it is smaller than Herring and Great Black-backed gulls. Young Laughing Gulls have brown backs and wings and tan heads. The very young birds have a wide black band along the top edge of their tails.

## Pelican

The pelican doesn't laugh; in fact, it rarely makes a sound. But it is an amusing bird to watch. It has an enormous bill; the bottom half has a large pouch for carrying fish, and it looks like it is smiling—a very large smile. Pelicans have large wings for the size of their bodies and they are powerful fliers.

The **Brown Pelican** is commonly seen along the south coast, sitting on bridges, piers, buoys, and the tops of telephone poles. They often fly along just a few inches above the water or in a line of other pelicans looking for fish in the water. When a Brown Pelican dives for food, it drops straight down into the water as if it had been shot from the sky. In some places they are quite tame and stay close to people, begging for food. The Brown Pelican has a light brown body and a white neck and head. In the summer, look for a dark red stripe along the back of its neck. The bill is gray and light orange. A young Brown Pelican has a white body with light brown wings and neck.

# Brown Pelican

*Body length:* 3 1/2 feet

# American White Pelican

*Body length:* 4 feet

This bird can't be confused with its brown cousin. It is pure white with black wing feathers and has an orange bill, legs, and feet. (Young **American White Pelicans** have gray bills and a gray neck.) They don't dive like the Brown Pelican. They feed by swimming slowly along in shallow water, scooping up fish with their large bills. Sometimes several White Pelicans fish together, forming a V just as they (and other birds) do when they migrate.

# Double-crested Cormorant

*Body length:* 27 inches

Fishermen call these birds "shags," perhaps because of the shaggy crest on top of their heads. The cormorant is a very good diver and underwater swimmer. It uses its wings and webbed feet to "fly" through the water chasing after fish, its favorite food.

You might have trouble getting a good look at this bird during feeding time. One minute the cormorant is floating along on the surface of the water, its head pointed up as if it were afraid of getting its bill wet. The next minute it disappears. It might be out of sight for several minutes before it pops to the surface, often far away from the spot where it dived.

Cormorants are friendly birds (with each other, that is), and you might see a large flock of them on the rocks offshore. They often sit with their wings stretched out to dry. Cormorants must dry their wings because they do not have natural oil in their feathers to shed water as other water birds do.

The **Double-crested Cormorant** is a large bird— about the size of a goose. The double crest on its head is hard to see, but this bird is not hard to identify. It has greenish-black feathers, black feet, a gray bill, and an orange patch on its chin.

Beginning bird watchers sometimes confuse the **Common Loon** with the cormorant. They are about the same size, and both birds sit low in the water with their heads pointed up. Both are very good divers and swimmers. In the winter, a young Double-crested Cormorant has almost the same coloring as a loon does. But there are ways to tell them apart. With its legs far back on its body, a loon is made for swimming, not walking. Unlike the cormorant, the loon hardly ever is seen on land.

In late spring, in summer, and in early fall, the loon is easily identified by its summer colors—a dark green

# Common Loon

*Body length:* 2 feet

head, a striped "collar," and rows of white spots on its dark back. The Common Loon spends the summer on lakes and ponds, where it is often heard at night making the spooky, laughing sound that gave this bird its name. The Common Loon really has four different calls that it uses to "talk" with other loons. During fall and winter, when the loon is seen most often on the coast, it is usually quiet.

125

# Mallard Duck

*Body length:*
16 inches

*female mallard*

*male mallard*

The **Mallard Duck** is another bird that lives on lakes and ponds as well as along the coast. You might see Mallards in a marsh or shallow cove, paddling along in a group made up of Mallards and other ducks. Mallards are often seen with their close cousin, the **American Black Duck.**

---

126

The male Mallard is easiest to identify. It has a shiny, green head; white neck band; rust-colored breast; white belly; and tan wings with a bright blue stripe. (The stripe looks like a blue patch when the Mallard is sitting in the water.) The female looks a lot like the American Black Duck, but she is a lighter shade of brown. Also, her wing stripe is blue like the male Mallard, not purple like the stripe of the American Black Duck. The Mallard has a very loud quack.

# American Black Duck

*Body length:* 16 inches

You might have to get up early in the morning to see this bird. The **Black Duck** is very shy (perhaps because it's a popular target for duck hunters), and it usually eats and travels at night. Still, the Black Duck is the most common wild duck on the Atlantic coast. If you can visit a bird sanctuary along the coast, you are very likely to see a Black Duck eating during the daytime.

The Black Duck is really dark brown, with a lighter brown head. It looks so much like a female Mallard that it is often called the Dusky Mallard or Black Mallard. The Black Duck is the same size as a Mallard and even has the same loud quack. But you can identify the Black Duck by its bright yellow bill and by the purple band with the narrow, white stripe it has along its wing.

Mallards and American Black Ducks are "surface feeders." They eat plants and sometimes bugs and small fish that they find on or near the surface of the water. These birds can be a funny sight while feeding. You might see one of these ducks paddling along, nibbling at the surface of the water. Suddenly it dips its head and the front of its body into the water to reach for food, leaving its tail sticking up in the air.

# Bufflehead

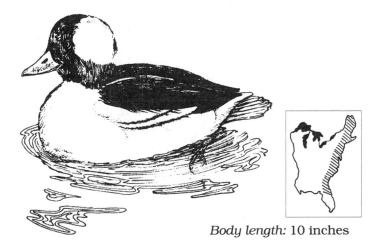

*Body length:* 10 inches

The **Bufflehead** is one of the smallest ducks on the Atlantic coast. Its markings make it easy to identify, too. The male Bufflehead is snowy white on its breast, stomach, and sides. It has a white patch, like a cap, that stretches from eye to eye on top of its dark green head. The top of its wings and body are black with white stripes. It is easiest to see the stripes when the bird is flying. The female Bufflehead is grayish white on the breast, stomach, and sides. She is dark gray everywhere else, but has a white patch on each cheek and a white band at the back of each wing near her body. Like other sea ducks, the Bufflehead has a plump body, a short neck, and a short tail. Winter is the best time to see this bird on the coast because it stays near lakes and rivers in the summer. In the winter, you often see large flocks of Buffleheads in saltwater rivers and in coves.

# Canada Goose

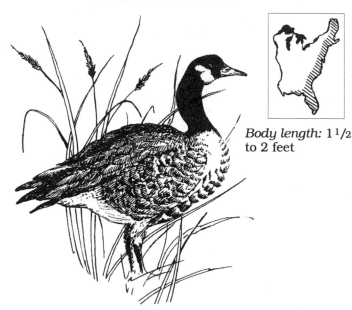

Body length: 1 1/2 to 2 feet

This is the most common goose, not only along the Atlantic coast, but in all of North America. The **Canada Goose** is large and it is easy to identify by the color and pattern of its feathers. Look for a gray body; a long, black neck; and a white band, which looks like a wide strap, under the goose's chin.

Like many birds, Canada Geese migrate. They fly to cooler places in the spring and to warmer places in the fall. Canada Geese migrate in groups (flocks)—from a few dozen birds to a hundred or more. When flying, they form the letter V in the air. You can often hear the geese coming before you see them, because they honk as if trying to get through a traffic jam. When they stop to rest, they often can be seen in fields near the water, grazing on grass just as cows do.

# Osprey

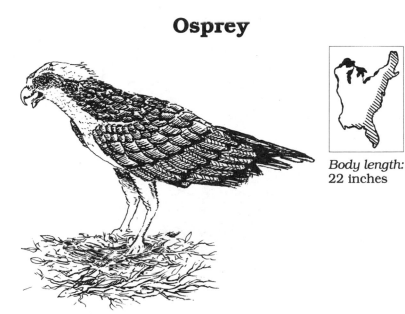

*Body length:*
22 inches

This large, fish-eating bird might be seen anywhere along the Atlantic coast, but it is most commonly seen in Florida, where it lives all year. Farther north, it is a summer resident. It also lives near lakes and rivers—anywhere the fishing is good. When the **Osprey** is flying, its tail is shaped like a fan, and the tips of its long wings (five and a half feet from tip to tip) are like fingers. It is white underneath and brown on top. The head is white, but there is a brown streak through the eye from its beak to its neck.

# Bald Eagle

*Body length:* 32 inches

This majestic bird was once endangered because there were pesticides in the dead fish it eats. A chemical called DDT changed the bird's body chemistry so that the eggs it laid had very thin shells that broke before the baby birds hatched. Since DDT has been banned to protect the environment, the eggs are hatching and there are more **Bald Eagles** on the Atlantic coast and elsewhere than there were ten years ago.

Bald Eagles are a thrilling sight to see. With their wingspan of nearly seven feet, they seem to fill the sky with their silent, graceful flight. They often soar high in the sky with their wings spread flat. They are easy to recognize by their white head and tail, charcoal-colored body, and yellow beak and feet.

Bald Eagles usually return to the same nest year after year. Their nests are enormous and can weigh as much as a ton. Bald Eagles are predators that eat rodents and other small animals. Like the Osprey, the Bald Eagle has strong talons that it uses to capture and carry its food.

# Red-winged Blackbird

*Body length:* 8 inches

This is a cheerful blackbird with bright orange and yellow patches on its shoulders. It is a familiar sight throughout the United States, but it is most common in marshlands and in fields that are near water. It has a long black bill and black feet. The **Red-winged Blackbird** seems to sing every time it lands and takes off—a loud, long, musical but slightly squeaky song that is easy to recognize.

# Seaside Sparrow

*Body length:* 6 inches

This is the only sparrow that lives only near the seashore. It is commonly seen in salt marshes and bushes along the Atlantic coast from New England to Florida. It is a perky little bird, mostly gray, with yellow and white streaks on its breast and a yellow line in front of each eye. It has a short, narrow tail and a long, gray bill that it uses to catch insects and small sea creatures, such as tiny crabs and snails.

# Appendix

You might already have some favorite places to visit when you go to the seashore. But part of the fun of exploring is finding new places. Here is a list of some special places along the Atlantic coast. The outdoor places listed below are for everyone to enjoy. Some charge a fee to visit; many do not. Some places are small; some are very large. Most have hiking trails along the coast, through salt marshes, sand dunes, seaside forests, and over rocks. Some have exhibits and programs about the environment. The places and the towns in which they are located are listed alphabetically under the state in which they are found. You can find out more about each place when you visit the area.

## Maine

Acadia National Park
Camden Hills State Park, Camden
Crescent Beach State Park, Cape Elizabeth
East Point Sanctuary, Biddeford
Ferry Beach State Park, Saco
Fox Island Tombolo, Popham Beach
Holbrook Island Sanctuary, Brooksville
Pemaquid Beach Park, Bristol
Petit Manan, Steuben
Popham Beach State Park, Phippsburg

## Maine

Popham Marsh, Popham
Prout's Neck Bird Sanctuary, Scarborough
Quoddy Head State Park, Lubec
Rachel Carson National Wildlife Refuge, Wells
Reid Beach, Georgetown
Roque Bluffs State Park, Roque Bluffs
Scarborough Beach State Park, Scarborough
Sohier Park, York
Two Lights State Park, Cape Elizabeth
Wolf Neck Woods State Park, Freeport

## New Hampshire

Hampton Beach State Park, Hampton Beach
Hampton Harbor Marsh, Hampton

## Massachusetts

Cape Cod National Seashore
Crane's Beach, Ipswich
Halibut Point Reservation, Rockport
Ipswich River Wildlife Sanctuary, Topsfield
Parker River National Wildlife Refuge, Newburyport
Salisbury Beach State Reservation, Salisbury Beach
Wellfleet Bay Wildlife Sanctuary, South Wellfleet
World's End Reservation, Hingham

## Rhode Island

Beavertail Point State Park, Jamestown
Burlingame State Park, Charlestown
Napatree Point, Watch Hill
Ninigret National Wildlife Refuge, Charlestown
Norman Bird Sanctuary, Middletown
Trustom Pond, South Kingston

## Connecticut

Barn Island Wildlife Management Area, Stonington
Bluff Point State Park, Groton
Hamonasset Beach State Park, Madison
Milford Point Sanctuary, Milford

# New York

Caumsett State Park, Lloyd Neck
Fire Island National Seashore, Shirly
Jamaica Bay Wildlife Refuge, New York City
Marshlands Conservatory, Rye
Nerrill Lake Nature Trail, East Hampton
Montauk Point State Park, Montauk
Orient Beach State Park, Orient
Welwyn Reserve, Glen Cove

# New Jersey

Brigantine National Wildlife Refuge, Oceanville
Cape May Bird Sanctuary, Cape May Point
Cape May Point State Park, Cape May Point
Carson's Inlet, Strathmore
Gateway National Recreational Area, Highlands
Island Beach State Park, Seaside Park
Long Beach Island, Oceanville
Stone Harbor Point, Stone Harbor

# Delaware

Beach Plum Island, Broadkill Beach
Bombay Hook National Wildlife Reserve, Smyrna
Cape Henlopen State Park, Lewes
Delaware Seashore State Park
Prime Hook National Wildlife Refuge, Milton
Woodland Beach Wildlife Area, Smyrna

# Maryland

Assateague Island National Seashore
Assateague Island State Park, Berlin
Calvert Cliffs State Park, Olivet
Chincoteague National Wildlife Refuge, Chincoteague
Eastern Neck National Wildlife Reserve, Rock Hall
Elk Neck State Park, North East
Jug Bay Natural Area, Upper Marlboro
Point Lookout State Park, Scotland
Sandy Point State Park, Annapolis

# Virginia
Back Bay National Wildlife Refuge, Virginia Beach
Jamestown Island, Jamestown
Mason Neck Wildlife Reserve, Lorton
Newport News City Park, Newport News
Northern Point Natural Reserve, Hampton
Ragged Island Wildlife Management Area, Newport News
Seashore State Park, Virginia Beach
Westmoreland State Park, Montross

# North Carolina
Cape Hatteras National Seashore
Croatan National Forest
Jockey's Ridge State Park, Nag's Head
Swanquarter National Wildlife Refuge
Theodore Roosevelt Natural Area State Park

# South Carolina
Cape Romain National Wildlife Refuge
Hunting Island State Park

# Georgia
Blackbeard Island National Wildlife Refuge and Wilderness
 Area
Cumberland Island National Seashore
Jekyll Island State Park
Ossabaw Island Heritage Park
R.J. Reynolds State Wildlife Refuge
Sapelo Natural Area and Estuary
Skidwaway Island State Park
Tybee National Wildlife Refuge
Wassaw National Wildlife Refuge
Wolf Island National Wildlife Refuge and Wilderness Area

# Florida
Biscayne National Park
Canaveral National Seashore
Everglades National Park
Lignumvitae Key State Botanical Site
Loxahatchee National Wildlife Refuge

# Glossary

**antenna** A small (sometimes long) thin animal part attached to the animal's head. Like a cat's whisker, the antenna helps the animal to "feel" or sense its surroundings. An animal that has an antenna always has two of them. The word for more than one antenna is *antennae*.

**alga** A primitive plant that has no real stems, roots, or leaves. Seaweed is a kind of alga.

**bay** In a lake or the ocean, a bay is a place along the shore where the water is quiet and protected from the wind and waves. A bay is sometimes called a *cove* or an *inlet*.

**bed** A group of sea creatures, such as mussels, that live together attached to rocks, mud, and each other. A bed of mussels is sometimes called a *colony* of mussels.

**bird sanctuary** An outdoor place where birds are protected by law from hunters who might disturb either the birds or their nests.

**camouflage** On an animal, coloring that helps it blend in with its environment. Camouflage helps an animal hide from other animals that might want to eat it.

**colony** A group of animals or plants living together. Barnacles and mussels live in colonies, sometimes called *beds*.

**cove** Another word for a bay or inlet.

**dune** A hill of sand that was made by the wind.

**environment** The surroundings where a plant or animal lives.

**eyespot** A spot on an animal that senses light or dark. It cannot see as an eye can.

**eyestalk** A stalk-like body part on a crab or other creature. The animal's eye is on top of the eyestalk.

**field mark** On a bird, the color of its feathers or of a body part. Field marks help people identify birds.

**fin** A thin body part on a fish that helps it to swim.

**flock** A group of birds or other animals.

**foot** The muscle that a mollusk uses to move itself from place to place.

**fragile** Easy to break.

**gill** The body part that allows some water creatures to breathe. Animals that have gills take oxygen from the water, just as animals with lungs take oxygen from the air.

**growth lines** Curved lines or ridges on a mollusk that show how the mollusk has grown. Growth lines on a mollusk are like growth rings on a tree.

**high-tide line** The place on the shore where the water is highest when the tide is in.

**hinge** On a two-shell mollusk, the place where the two shells are attached.

**holdfast** The part of a seaweed that attaches the seaweed to a rock or shell. The holdfast on seaweed is like the root of a land plant.

**inlet** Another word for a cove or bay.

140

**larva** The young form of an animal after it has hatched from an egg and before it is an adult. Butterflies, frogs, and barnacles are some animals that begin life as a larva. Sometimes the larva looks like a tiny worm.

**low-tide line** The place on the shore where the water is lowest when the tide is out.

**marsh** Land that is flat and partly covered with water. A marsh has plants, usually tall grass, growing around and in it. A *salt marsh* is a marsh that is near or connected to the ocean. The saltwater of a salt marsh rises and falls with the tides.

**migrate** To move from one place to another as the seasons of the year change. Many birds and some ocean-living animals migrate.

**mollusk** A water animal that has a soft body covered by a hard shell.

**muscle scar** The mark on the inside of a two-shelled mollusk that shows where the foot, or muscle, was attached.

**pesticide** A chemical used to kill insects and rodents. Farmers use pesticides to protect their gardens, but pesticides can harm or kill other animals, too.

**pincer** The grabbing claw of an animal, such as a crab or lobster.

**predator** An animal that eats another animal.

**prey** An animal that is eaten by another animal.

**regenerate** To replace a body part that has been destroyed or removed. Starfish can regenerate rays and lobsters can regenerate claws.

**ribs** The lines or ridges on the outside of shells.

**seaweed** Plants that grow in the sea.

**shorebird** A bird that lives along the seashore.

**surf** Ocean waves that crash, or "break," on the shore.

**tentacle** A body part that a water animal uses to grab food or to hold on to objects. Jellyfish and sea anemones are among the animals that have tentacles.

**tide chart** A list that shows when the tide will be high and when the tide will be low.

**tide pool** A pool of seawater left in the rocks or sand when the tide goes out.

**tides** The rising and falling of the ocean that takes place twice each day. The tides are caused by the changing position of the earth in relation to the sun and moon.

**tube foot** One of the many small body parts on the bottom of some water animals. The animal uses its tube feet for eating and for moving from place to place. On many animals with tube feet, each tube foot has a tiny suction cup on the end.

**undertow** Water current that moves back toward the open sea when waves break on the shore. Sometimes undertow is very strong and dangerous. It can knock you down and pull you out into the deep water.

**wave** A moving ridge on the surface of the water.

# Checklist

As you see each plant, animal, and shell, make a check mark on the list below. Within each group, the names are listed in alphabetical order. The page numbers show where to find each plant or animal in this guidebook. You might want to write down where you found each one. For example, you could name the state, town, beach, or park. When you have checked off everything on the list, cut out the Sea-Searcher's Award and hang it on the wall or put it in your scrapbook.

## Sea Creatures

| | page | where found |
|---|---|---|
| ❑ American Lobster | 16 | _____ |
| Barnacle | | |
| ❑ Bay | 30 | |
| ❑ Ivory | 30 | _____ |
| ❑ Large Rock | 29 | _____ |
| ❑ Little Gray | 30 | _____ |
| ❑ Northern Rock | 31 | _____ |
| ❑ Big-eyed Beach Flea | 28 | _____ |
| ❑ Cayenne Keyhole Limpet | 32 | _____ |
| Chiton | | |
| ❑ Common Eastern | 35 | _____ |
| ❑ Red Northern | 35 | _____ |
| ❑ Clam Worm | 42 | _____ |

| Crab | page | where found |
|---|---|---|
| ❏ Arrow | 24 | _____ |
| ❏ Atlantic Mole | 24 | _____ |
| ❏ Atlantic Rock | 18 | _____ |
| ❏ Blue | 22 | _____ |
| ❏ Common Spider | 19 | _____ |
| ❏ Ghost | 21 | _____ |
| ❏ Green | 21 | _____ |
| ❏ Hermit, Acadian | 26 | _____ |
| ❏ Hermit, Long-clawed | 26 | _____ |
| ❏ Jonah | 19 | _____ |
| ❏ Lady | 18 | _____ |
| ❏ Sand Fiddler | 20 | _____ |
| ❏ Stone | 23 | _____ |
| ❏ Wharf | 23 | _____ |
| ❏ Horseshoe Crab | 27 | _____ |

Jellyfish
| | | |
|---|---|---|
| ❏ Cannonball (Jellyball) | 38 | _____ |
| ❏ Lion's Mane | 37 | _____ |
| ❏ Moon | 36 | _____ |
| ❏ Sea Nettle | 37 | _____ |
| ❏ Upside-down | 38 | _____ |
| ❏ Leafy Paddle Worm | 41 | |

Limpet
| | | |
|---|---|---|
| ❏ Atlantic Plate | 32 | _____ |
| ❏ Cayenne Keyhole | 32 | _____ |
| ❏ Limulus Leech | 42 | _____ |
| ❏ Mussel Colony | 33 | |

Sand Dollar
| | | |
|---|---|---|
| ❏ Common | 14 | _____ |
| ❏ Keyhole Urchin | 15 | _____ |
| ❏ Six-hole Urchin | 15 | _____ |

Sea Anemone
| | | |
|---|---|---|
| ❏ Frilled | 40 | _____ |
| ❏ Ghost | 40 | _____ |
| ❏ Lined | 40 | _____ |
| ❏ Striped | 41 | _____ |

|  | page | where found |
|---|---|---|
| Sea Urchin | | |
| ❑ Atlantic Purple | 12 | _____ |
| ❑ Green Sea | 13 | _____ |
| ❑ Snail | 33 | _____ |
| Sponge | | |
| ❑ Crumb-of-Bread | 44 | _____ |
| ❑ Finger | 44 | _____ |
| ❑ Red Beard | 44 | _____ |
| Starfish | | |
| ❑ Blood Star | 10 | _____ |
| ❑ Cushion Star | 9 | _____ |
| ❑ Forbes's Common Sea Star | 11 | _____ |
| ❑ Northern Sea Star | 11 | _____ |
| ❑ Slender Sea Star | 10 | _____ |
| ❑ Smooth Sun Star | 11 | _____ |
| ❑ Thorny Sea Star | 9 | _____ |
| ❑ Two-gilled Blood Worm | 42 | _____ |

## Insects

| | | |
|---|---|---|
| ❑ American Horse Fly | 104 | _____ |
| ❑ Deer Fly | 104 | _____ |
| ❑ Eastern Sand Wasp | 103 | _____ |
| ❑ Field Cricket | 107 | _____ |
| ❑ Saltmarsh Mosquito | 105 | _____ |
| ❑ Seaside Grasshopper | 106 | _____ |
| Tick | | |
| ❑ Deer Tick | 106 | _____ |
| ❑ Dog Tick | 105 | _____ |

## Shells to Collect

| | | |
|---|---|---|
| ❑ Alphabet Cone | 61 | _____ |
| ❑ Angel Wing | 66 | _____ |
| ❑ Angulate Wentletrap | 60 | _____ |
| ❑ Apple Murex | 59 | _____ |
| ❑ Atlantic Dogwinkle | 49 | _____ |
| ❑ Atlantic Oyster Drill | 49 | _____ |

| | page | where found |
|---|---|---|
| **Mussel** | | |
| ❑ Atlantic Ribbed | 76 | _____ |
| ❑ Blue | 76 | _____ |
| ❑ Northern Horse | 75 | _____ |
| ❑ Northern Cardita | 70 | _____ |
| ❑ Oyster Drill | 49 | _____ |
| **Pen Shell** | | |
| ❑ Saw-toothed | 79 | _____ |
| ❑ Stiff | 78 | _____ |
| **Periwinkle** | | |
| ❑ Common | 50 | _____ |
| ❑ Marsh | 50 | _____ |
| ❑ Northern Yellow | 50 | _____ |
| ❑ Pink Conch | 64 | _____ |
| ❑ Ponderous Ark | 67 | _____ |
| **Quahog** | | |
| ❑ Northern | 74 | _____ |
| ❑ Ocean | 75 | _____ |
| **Sand Dollar** | | |
| ❑ Common | 14 | _____ |
| ❑ Keyhole Urchin | 15 | _____ |
| ❑ Six-holed Keyhole | 15 | _____ |
| **Scallop** | | |
| ❑ Atlantic Bay | 78 | _____ |
| ❑ Atlantic Deep Sea | 77 | _____ |
| ❑ Scotch Bonnet | 58 | _____ |
| ❑ Shark Eye | 53 | _____ |
| ❑ Sunray Venus | 65 | _____ |
| ❑ True Tulip | 62 | _____ |
| ❑ Turkey Wing | 65 | _____ |
| ❑ West Indian Worm Shell | 60 | _____ |
| **Whelk** | | |
| ❑ Channelled | 53 | _____ |
| ❑ Eastern Mud | 51 | _____ |
| ❑ Knobbed | 53 | _____ |
| ❑ New England Basket | 51 | _____ |

## Seashore Plants    page    where found

*In the Sea*

| | page | where found |
|---|---|---|
| ❑ Chenille Weed | 88 | _____ |
| ❑ Dulse | 84 | _____ |
| ❑ Green Thread Algae | 82 | _____ |
| ❑ Irish Moss | 88 | _____ |
| ❑ Kelp | 84 | _____ |
| ❑ Knotted Wrack | 83 | _____ |
| ❑ Link Confetti | 87 | _____ |
| ❑ Purple Laver | 86 | _____ |
| ❑ Rockweed | 83 | _____ |
| ❑ Sea Colander | 85 | _____ |
| ❑ Sea Grass | 87 | _____ |
| ❑ Sea Lettuce | 86 | _____ |
| ❑ Sea Potato | 89 | _____ |

*Near the Sea*

| | page | where found |
|---|---|---|
| ❑ American Beach Grass | 91 | _____ |
| ❑ Bayberry | 100 | _____ |
| ❑ Beach Heather | 97 | _____ |
| ❑ Beach Pea | 98 | _____ |
| ❑ Beach Rose | 99 | _____ |
| ❑ Dusty Miller | 96 | _____ |
| ❑ Eelgrass | 90 | _____ |
| ❑ Glasswort | 95 | _____ |
| Mangrove | | _____ |
| ❑ Black | 102 | _____ |
| ❑ Red | 101 | _____ |
| ❑ White | 102 | _____ |
| ❑ Reed Grass | 92 | _____ |
| ❑ Saltmeadow Cordgrass | 94 | _____ |
| ❑ Saltmarsh Bullrush | 92 | _____ |
| ❑ Saltmarsh Cordgrass | 93 | _____ |
| ❑ Sea Lavender | 95 | _____ |
| ❑ Sea Oats | 91 | _____ |
| ❑ Sea Rocket | 96 | _____ |
| ❑ Seaside Goldenrod | 98 | _____ |
| ❑ Spike Grass | 94 | _____ |
| ❑ Turtle Grass | 90 | _____ |

## Shorebirds

| Shorebirds | page | where found |
|---|---|---|
| ❏ American Black Duck | 127 | _____ |
| ❏ Bald Eagle | 132 | _____ |
| ❏ Bufflehead | 129 | _____ |
| ❏ Canada Goose | 130 | _____ |
| ❏ Common Loon | 125 | _____ |
| ❏ Double-crested Cormorant | 123 | _____ |
| ❏ Great Blue Heron | 110 | _____ |
| ❏ Great White Egret | 111 | _____ |
| Gulls | | |
| ❏ Great Black-backed | 119 | _____ |
| ❏ Herring | 119 | _____ |
| ❏ Laughing | 120 | _____ |
| ❏ Mallard Duck | 126 | _____ |
| ❏ Osprey | 131 | _____ |
| Pelican | | |
| ❏ American White | 122 | _____ |
| ❏ Brown | 121 | _____ |
| ❏ Red-winged Blackbird | 133 | _____ |
| Sandpiper | | |
| ❏ Least | 113 | _____ |
| ❏ Purple | 114 | _____ |
| ❏ Sanderling | 115 | _____ |
| ❏ Semipalmated | 114 | _____ |
| ❏ Spotted | 115 | _____ |
| ❏ Seaside Sparrow | 134 | _____ |
| ❏ Snowy Egret | 112 | _____ |
| Tern | | |
| ❏ Caspian | 116 | _____ |
| ❏ Common | 117 | _____ |
| ❏ Forster's | 117 | _____ |
| ❏ Roseate | 118 | _____ |

# About the Author

**Judith Hansen** grew up in Maine's Lincoln County and has spent many hours exploring the coastal and inland waterways of the Northeast. A graduate of the University of Maine, she taught primary school in Boston and in Williamsburg, Virginia; nature study always figured prominently in her classroom activities. Ms. Hansen began her writing career in 1972, working variously as a journalist, publicist, and marketing communications consultant over the next ten years. She now lives in Kennebunk, Maine, where she publishes *The Tourist News*, a three-season newspaper for visitors in southern Maine. *Seashells in My Pocket* is her first book.

# About the Artist

**Donna Sabaka** majored in Fine Arts at Bowling Green State University in Ohio and has studied at the Cleveland Art Institute and the University of Southern Maine. Her illustrations have appeared in several books for children and adults. Ms. Sabaka has a gallery in Kennebunkport and has exhibited her work in many local and regional shows. As a water colorist, she specializes in florals and seascapes. Ms. Sabaka lives in Arundel, Maine.

# About the AMC

The Appalachian Mountain Club is where recreation and conservation meet. More than 64,000 members have joined the AMC to pursue their interests in hiking, canoeing, skiing, walking, rock climbing, bicycling, camping, kayaking, and backpacking, and—at the same time—to help safeguard the environment in which these activities are possible.

Since it was founded in 1876, the Club has been at the forefront of the environmental protection movement. By cofounding several of New England's leading environmental organizations, and working in coalition with these and many more groups, the AMC has influenced legislation and public opinion.

Volunteers in each chapter lead hundreds of outdoor activities and excursions and offer introductory instruction in back-country sports. The AMC Education Department offers members and the public a wide range of workshops, from introductory camping to the intensive Mountain Leadership School taught on the trails of the White Mountains.

The most recent efforts in the AMC conservation program include river protection, Northern Forest Lands policy, support for the American Heritage Trust, Sterling Forest (NY) preservation, and support for the Clean Air Act.

The AMC's research department focuses on the forces affecting the ecosystem, including ozone levels, acid rain and fog, climate change, rare flora and habitat protection, and air quality and visibility.

The AMC Volunteer Trails Program is active through-out the AMC's twelve chapters and maintains over 1,200 miles of trails, including 350 miles of the Appalachian Trail. Under the supervision of experienced leaders, hundreds of volunteers spend from one afternoon to two weeks working on trail projects.

The Club operates eight alpine huts in the White Mountains that provide shelter, bunks and blankets, and hearty meals for hikers. Pinkham Notch Visitor Center, at the foot of Mt. Washington, is base camp to the adventurous and the ideal location for individuals and families new to outdoor recreation. Comfortable bunkrooms, mountain hospitality, and home-cooked, family-style meals make Pinkham Notch Visitor Center a fun and affordable choice for lodging.

At the AMC headquarters in Boston, the bookstore and information center stock the entire line of AMC publications, as well as other trail and river guides, maps, reference materials, and the latest articles on conservation issues. Also available from the bookstore or by subscription is *Appalachia*, the country's oldest mountaineering and conservation journal.

We invite you to join the Appalachian Mountain Club and share the benefits of membership. Every member receives *Appalachia Bulletin*, the membership magazine that, ten times a year, brings you news about environmental issues and AMC projects, plus listings of outdoor activities, workshops, excursions, and volunteer opportunities. Members also enjoy discounts on AMC books, maps, educational workshops, and guided hikes, as well as reduced fees at all AMC huts and lodges in Massachusetts and New Hampshire. To join today, call 617-523-0636; or write to: AMC, 5 Joy Street, Boston, MA 02108.

# Sea-Searcher's Award

PRINT YOUR NAME HERE

has found and identified all the animals, shells, and plants described and illustrated in *Seashells in My Pocket*

DATE

ISBN 1-878239-15-5